THE INSIDER'S

DOING THE DBQ

AP U.S. HISTORY
2023 EXAM

THE ESSENTIAL DBQ GUIDE

by LARRY KRIEGER

THE INSIDER'S DOING THE DBQ
AP U.S. HISTORY 2023 Exam
THE ESSENTIAL DBQ GUIDE

by LARRY KRIEGER

ISBN: 978-1-7368182-6-8
An INSIDER TEST PREP publication of Larry Prep LLC
Art Direction & Design by Station16 (Station16 LLC)

For more Insider resources visit
www.InsiderTestPrep.com

TABLE OF CONTENTS

ABOUT THE AUTHOR

Larry Krieger earned his B.A. and M.A.T. from the University of North Carolina at Chapel Hill and his M.A. from Wake Forest University. In a career spanning more than four decades, Mr. Krieger taught in urban, rural, and suburban public high schools in North Carolina and New Jersey. He taught a variety of AP subjects including U.S. History, Art History, European History, and American Government. Mr. Krieger has written popular books in all of these subjects.

Mr. Krieger's AP US History courses are renowned for their energetic presentations, commitment to scholarship, and dedication to helping students achieve high AP exam scores. Over 90 percent of Mr. Krieger's APUSH students have scored 5s with the remainder scoring 4s. Mr. Krieger has never had an AP student score a 1 or 2.

ACKNOWLEDGEMENTS

Books do not write themselves. They require the work of a dedicated and creative team.

The typed manuscript must be proofed and assembled into an attractive, well-designed book. As always, Station16 more than met this challenge. Brenton played a key leadership role. He developed a distinctive design, offered valuable advice, and as always created an original cover. David proofed each page, Stacy shaped the manuscript into flowing layouts, and Brenton managed the project to a successful conclusion.

I would like to thank three APUSH teachers who played a role in inspiring this book. Carl Florczyk teaches at Freeburg Community High School in Freeburg, Illinois. Carl's suggestions included using charts to help students organize their thoughts. Alexander Gonzalez teaches at Blake High School in Tampa, Florida. Alex's enthusiasm and strategic insights helped inspire and guide me. And finally, Andrew Offineer is the Social Studies Department Chair at Mountain View High School in Stafford, Virginia. Andrew contributed the idea of using the "Although... in the end" method of writing a sophisticated thesis.

INTRODUCTION

Preparing for the 2023 APUSH exam will be a formidable challenge. The current situation has forced schools to use a combination of in-class, distant learning, and hybrid approaches. In addition, an unusually harsh winter has forced many districts to cancel classes. The loss of class time is making it difficult for teachers to complete the required APUSH curriculum.

THE DBQ CHALLENGE

The Document-Based Essay Question (DBQ) poses a particular challenge for many APUSH students. This is not a surprise. The DBQ format requires students to analyze seven primary source documents and then use these excerpts to compose a coherent essay that responds to a difficult prompt.

The College Board recommends that students devote 60 minutes to the DBQ. This pressure-packed assignment produces low average scores. The DBQ scoring rubric awards students 7 possible points. Between 2017 and 2019, average scores ranged from a low of 2.22 to a "high" of 2.54. Remember, a 7 is a perfect score. Low DBQ scores make it very difficult for students to earn overall APUSH scores of a 5 or 4.

A BOLD NEW APPROACH

My long experience helping students prepare for the DBQ essay led me to create a bold new approach to doing the DBQ. This book provides you with 12 practice DBQs. Each DBQ is followed by an annotated essay enabling you to pinpoint how the essay fulfilled rubric requirements. The annotated sample essays are based upon insights from featured essays on AP Central and from best practices recommended by experienced DBQ readers.

A STRATEGIC ORGANIZATION

The Insider's Doing the DBQ is divided into 4 units. The first unit begins by providing you with basic information about the DBQ scoring rubric. Chapter 2 then identifies and explains ten key strategies that will help you write effective essays. Chapter 3 shows you how to apply these strategies to a sample DBQ.

The second unit focuses on the historical reasoning process of continuity and change. This critical thinking skill generates the majority of all DBQ prompts. The introductory chapter discusses the importance of this historical thinking skill and shows you how to design an organizational chart for change and continuity DBQs. Chapters 5 - 8 provide you with an opportunity to practice analyzing and writing change and continuity DBQ essays. These chapters use carefully selected prompts designed to provide a review of key developments in African American history and the Cold War.

The third unit focuses on the historical reasoning process of causation. This critical thinking skill generates about a fourth of the DBQ prompts. The introductory chapter discusses the importance of this historical thinking skill and shows you how to design an organizational chart for causation DBQs. Chapters 14 - 16 provide you with an opportunity to practice analyzing and writing causation DBQ essays. The chapters cover such key topics as the effects of the rise of mass democracy, and the causes of the rise of the environmental and women's rights movements.

A UNIQUE PLAN B STRATEGY

Your Plan A should always be to begin by carefully reading the prompt and the seven documents. But what if you are unprepared for the prompt and don't understand all the documents? Our fourth unit introduces and illustrates a unique Plan B that will help you earn 4 of the 7 rubric points.

Chapter 13 introduces and explains the Plan B strategy. The chapter then provides an illustrative Plan B annotated essay. Chapters 14, 15 and 16 give you additional practice writing Plan B essays on Western Expansion, immigration, and foreign policy.

PRACTICE, PRACTICE, PRACTICE

Practice is essential. Your DBQ essay will not magically write itself. The strategies and examples in this book will help build your competence and confidence. YOU CAN DO IT!

THE 2023 APUSH EXAM FORMAT

THE EXAM: 3 HOURS AND 15 MINUTES LONG

1. Multiple Choice: 55 questions, 55 minutes, 40 percent of the exam score.
2. Short Answer: 3 questions, 40 minutes, 20 percent of the exam score. The first two short answer questions are mandatory. However, you have a choice between two prompts for the third question.
3. Document-Based Question: 1 question, 60 minutes, 25 percent of the exam score.
4. Long Essay: 1 question, 40 minutes, 15 percent of the exam score. You will have a choice among three prompts for your long essay.

THE APUSH SCALE

Many students assume the APUSH exam contains 100 points and that they need 90 points for a 5, 80 points for a 4, and 70 points for a 3. This common belief is incorrect. The APUSH exam actually contains 140 points. On the 2019 exam students needed 106 points for a 5, 90 points for a 4, and 72 points for a 3. Here is the official APUSH exam score conversion chart for the 2019 APUSH exam:

SCORE RANGE	AP SCORE	MINIMUM PERCENT CORRECT
106–140	5	76 percent
90–105	4	65 percent
72–89	3	52 percent
53–71	2	38 percent
0–52	1	0–37 percent

This chart is not a misprint. You can earn a 3 by correctly answering just 52 percent of the questions, a 4 by answering 65 percent of the questions, and a 5 by answering 76 percent of the questions.

The APUSH scale underscores the importance of the strategic approach used in this book. You do not have to memorize information in a textbook or a series of YouTube videos. Instead, you can achieve a high score by becoming familiar with the strategies and annotated essays presented in this book.

UNIT I
INTRODUCING THE DBQ

CHAPTER 1
BASIC INFORMATION

MASTERING THE DOCUMENT-BASED ESSAY QUESTION (DBQ)

After completing the short-answer questions, you will have a well-deserved 10-minute break. When you return to your desk, your exam will resume with the document-based question (DBQ).

The DBQ is an essay question requiring you to analyze and interpret 7 primary source documents. The documents are taken from letters, newspaper articles, speeches, diaries, and official decrees. In addition, the DBQ can include a political cartoon, map, or graph.

The College Board recommends that you begin your DBQ by devoting about 15 minutes to reading the documents, organizing your thoughts, crafting a thesis, and creating a topical outline. Once you have completed these tasks you should begin writing your essay. The College Board recommends that you devote about 45 minutes to writing your DBQ.

IMPORTANCE

The DBQ can earn up to 7 rubric points. Each rubric point is worth 5 exam points. Thus, a perfect score of 7 is worth 35 points, or 25 percent of your total exam score. It is important to remember that earning 3 of the 7 possible rubric points will keep you on pace to score a 3. Scoring 4 of the 7 possible points will keep you close to the pace you need to score a 4. And finally, scoring 5 of the 7 possible points will keep you on pace to earn a 5.

THE DBQ SCORING RUBRIC

A. The All-Important Thesis – 1 Point

1. Everyone agrees that a well-constructed thesis is essential for a strong essay. Don't be intimidated by the word "thesis." A thesis is the position or argument you are advancing to answer the DBQ prompt.
2. Your thesis must consist of one or more sentences located in one place. College Board readers strongly recommend that you place your thesis in your opening paragraph.
3. Your thesis should clearly state the arguments your essay will support.

B. Contextualization – 1 Point

1. History is not a series of unconnected events. Like the experiences in your life, historical events occur in a setting. Contextualization refers to the broader historical context that is relevant to your DBQ prompt.
2. The historical setting establishes the stage for your DBQ essay. Readers expect your contextualization paragraph to follow your thesis statement.
3. Avoid a "Star Wars" opening statement in which you take your readers on a journey to a historic event that took place in the distant past. Instead, pick a historic turning point closest to the starting date in your prompt and use it as an entry point.
4. Your contextualization statement should focus on the big themes and ideas that have influenced the issue in the DBQ prompt.

C. Document Use – First Point

1. The first document-use point is a gift from the College Board. Don't refuse it. All you have to do is accurately describe the contents of THREE documents and relate them to the topic posed by the DBQ prompt.
2. You can do it! Remember, a thesis statement followed by a contextualization paragraph is worth 10 exam points. The first document use point will add 5 points to your total. Fifteen points is 20 percent of the 75 points you need to score a 3!

D. Document Use – Second Point

1. The DBQ rubric awards a second document-use point for using the contents of 6 of the 7 documents. However, there is a catch: If you simply quote a document or summarize its contents you won't receive the second point.

2. So how do you earn the second document-use point? The test writers selected each of the seven documents for a reason. To earn the second point you must use the contents of 6 of the 7 documents to support your thesis.

3. Many graders recommend that you use all 7 documents. There is no penalty for misusing a document. If you misuse one document but correctly use six documents, you will receive the second document-use point.

E. Evidence Beyond the Documents – 1 point

1. The 7 documents do not cover all the possible relevant events, ideas, trends, and perspectives. The DBQ rubric will reward you with a point for including evidence that is not found in the documents.

2. The evidence cannot be a random fact that you "drop" into your essay. Instead, the evidence must advance your argument.

3. College Board readers recommend that you do not rely on a single example of outside evidence. Instead they recommend that you "flood your essay with historical evidence."

4. Your outside evidence must be relevant. That is, it must fall within the chronological period established by your DBQ prompt.

F. Analysis of Sources – 1 point

1. Each of your documents can be analyzed in four ways. First, by establishing its historic setting. Second, by determining the author's point of view. Third, by identifying the document's purpose. And finally, by pinpointing the document's intended audience.

2. The DBQ rubric awards 1 point for correctly identifying and analyzing the historic situation, point of view, purpose, OR intended audience for THREE of the documents. It is very important to remember the capitalized words OR and THREE!

3. Many College Board readers believe that identifying the historic situation is the most straightforward and therefore the easiest of the four document characteristics. You should be able to explain the historic situation for each document in a sentence or two.

G. Complex Understanding – 1 point

1. The complexity point is by far the most difficult rubric point to earn. In 2019, College Board readers awarded this point to less than 5 percent of the 501,530 DBQ essays.

2. The complexity point is awarded to essays that demonstrate a complex understanding of the historical development that is the focus of the DBQ prompt.

3. DBQ questions are written to invite sophisticated responses. A sophisticated response would examine more than one cause or consequence of an event. It would also recognize the presence of both continuity and change in a historic era.

4. DBQ readers are especially looking for your ability to see relationships among the 7 documents. For example, try to group documents that have similar viewpoints. Also be on the lookout for documents that corroborate, qualify, or modify your argument.

5. The complexity point does require thoughtful analysis. Don't give up. The complexity point may be elusive, but it is not impossible!

SEVEN IMPORTANT DO'S AND DON'TS

1. Use the reading period to carefully evaluate the prompt and each of the 7 documents. Don't begin your essay until you have a historically defensible thesis. Remember, no wind favors a ship without a destination. The thesis statement is the wind powering your essay!

2. Use short quotes from your documents to illustrate key points. Don't use long quotes.

3. Always strive to analyze and evaluate the documents. Don't summarize the documents.

4. Try to provide evidence beyond the documents that develops a key point that is not contained in the 7 documents. Don't "drop in" a name or event.

5. Use documentary evidence in your body paragraphs. Avoid using documents in your thesis statement.

6. Do write a clear and concise thesis. Don't underline your thesis. Readers are trained to look for it in your opening paragraph. Many readers recommend that you also write a concluding paragraph that briefly restates your thesis. A concise conclusion ties your essay together by providing a clear statement of your thesis.

7. Do write a full and complete essay. But don't worry about your essay's length or your number of paragraphs. There is no prescribed length and readers do not count the number of paragraphs.

CHAPTER 2
A SAMPLE DBQ: ANALYSIS AND STRATEGIES

The DBQ is a sophisticated, free-response question. Your APUSH exam will include one 60-minute DBQ. Your assignment will be to analyze and interpret seven primary source documents. Don't panic! You will not be tested on information from 1491 to 1754 (Periods 1 and 2) or from 1980 to the present (Period 9).

Practice is the key to performing well on the DBQ. This chapter begins with a sample DBQ. It then explains and illustrates ten strategies that can be applied to any DBQ.

PROMPT

Evaluate the extent of change in ideas about American independence from 1763 to 1776.

DOCUMENT 1

Source: British Order in Council, 1763.

We, the Commissioners of your Majesty's Treasury, beg leave humbly to represent to your Majesty that having taken into consideration the present state of the duties of customs imposed on your Majesty's subjects in America and the West Indies, we find that the revenue arising therefrom is very small and inconsiderable,...and is not yet sufficient to defray a fourth part of the expense necessary for collecting it. We observe with concern that through neglect, connivance, and fraud, not only is revenue impaired, but the commerce of the colonies diverted from its natural course...[This revenue] is more indispensable when the military establishment necessary for maintaining these colonies requires a large revenue to support it, and when their vast increase in territory and population makes the proper regulation of their trade of immediate necessity.

DOCUMENT 2

Source: The Virginia House of Burgesses, The Virginia Resolutions on the Stamp Act, 1765.

Resolved, that the taxation of the people by themselves, or by persons chosen by themselves to represent them, who can only know what taxes the people are able to bear, or the easiest method of raising them, and must themselves be affected by every tax laid on the people, is the only security against burdensome taxation, and the distinguishing characteristic of British freedom, without which the ancient constitution cannot exist.

Resolved, that his Majesty's liege people of this ancient colony have enjoyed the right of being thus governed by their own Assembly in the article of taxes and internal police, and that the same have never been forfeited, or any other way yielded up, but have been constantly recognized by the king and people of Great Britain.

DOCUMENT 3

Source: Mather Byles, renowned Boston Loyalist minister, question posed March 1770.

They call me a brainless Tory; but tell me, my young friend: Which is better – to be ruled by one tyrant three thousand miles away or by three thousand tyrants not a mile away?

DOCUMENT 4

Source: Samuel Adams, The Rights of the Colonists, 1772.

All men have a right to remain in a state of nature as long as they please; and in case of intolerable oppression, civil or religious, to leave the society they belong to, and enter into another. When men enter into society, it is by voluntary consent; and they have a right to demand and insist upon the performance of such conditions and previous limitations as form an equitable original compact…

The natural liberty of man is to be free from any superior power on earth, and not to be under the will or legislative authority of man, but only to have the law of nature for his rule.

DOCUMENT 5

Source: Joseph Galloway, "A Plan of a Proposed Union Between Great Britain and the Colonies", proposal debated and then rejected by the First Continental Congress, 1774.

That a British and American legislature, for regulating the administration of the general affairs of America, be proposed and established in America., including all the said colonies; within, and under which government, each colony shall retain its present constitution, and powers of regulating and governing its own internal police, in all cases whatsoever.

That the said government be administered by a President General, to be appointed by the King and a Grand Council, to be chosen by the representatives of the people of the several colonies, in their respective assemblies, once in every three years.

DOCUMENT 6

Source: In "Plain English," a Loyalist describes the reign of "lawless mobs," 1775.

Some of these people, who from a sense of their duty to the king, and a reverence for his laws, have behaved quietly and peaceably; and for which reason they have been deprived of their liberty, abused in their persons, and suffered such barbarous cruelties, insults, and indignities, besides the loss of their property, by the hands of lawless mobs and riots, as would have been disgraceful even for savages to have committed. The courts of justice being shut up in most parts of the province [Massachusetts], and the justices of those courts compelled by armed force, headed by some of your Congress, to refrain from doing their duties, at present it is rendered impracticable for those sufferers to obtain redress...

DOCUMENT 7

Source: John Adams, Letters of John Adams, Addressed to his Wife, July 3, 1776

The hopes of reconciliation, which were fondly entertained by multitudes of honest and well meaning, though weak and mistaken people, have been gradually and, at last, totally extinguished. Time has been given for the whole people maturely to consider the great question of independence, and to ripen their judgment, dissipate their fears, and allure their hopes, by discussing it in newspapers and pamphlets, by debating it in assemblies, conventions, committees of safety and inspection, in town and county meetings, as well as in private conversations, so that the whole people, in every colony of the thirteen, have now adopted it as their own act....

I am well aware of the toil, and blood, and treasure, that it will cost us to maintain this Declaration, and support and defend these States. Yes, through all the gloom, I can see the rays of ravishing light and glory. I can see that the end is more than worth all the means. And that posterity will triumph in that day's transaction.

STRATEGY 1
ANALYZE THE PROMPT

Begin by carefully analyzing the prompt. Each DBQ prompt is designed to answer the following three key questions:

1. What historical thinking skill is being assessed?
2. What topic are you asked to address?
3. What are the chronological boundaries of the essay prompt?

Our sample prompt provides clear answers to each of these three questions. The phrase "evaluate the extent of change" tells you that our sample DBQ will focus on the historical thinking skill of describing and explaining patterns of continuity and change. Your essay should address the "change in ideas about American independence." And finally, the prompt requires you to focus on the time period between 1763 and 1776.

STRATEGY 2
EXAMINE EACH DOCUMENT

Your next step is to read, analyze, and evaluate the seven documents. It is important to note that Document 7 concludes the DBQ by providing a letter John Adams wrote to his wife on the eve of the Declaration of Independence. Adams forcefully declared that "the hopes for reconciliation" with Great Britain are "at last, totally extinguished." As you read Documents 1 – 6 consider what ideas caused Adams and other Patriots to embrace the idea of independence.

STRATEGY 3
WRITE A COMBO OPENING PARAGRAPH

The 2021 DBQ scoring rubric awards 1 point for a thesis and 1 point for contextualization. Since the thesis must appear in either your first or last paragraph, one strategy is to write an introductory paragraph that combines contextualization with your thesis.

Contextualization is a big word for an easy concept. In our sample DBQ, contextualization applies to the historic setting in 1763. At that time the British and their American colonists were celebrating a glorious victory in the French and Indian War. While the Americans rejoiced and looked forward to enjoying a new era of peace and prosperity, somber British leaders faced an enormous national debt. The financial crisis forced the British government to shift its economic policy by ending the period of salutary neglect, enforcing the Navigation Acts, and enacting new taxes to raise revenue.

Your opening paragraph can condense this contextual information into 3 to 4 sentences. To complete your Combo Paragraph, now transition to your thesis statement. Carefully read each of the 7 documents in our sample DBQ. Each document illustrates a key development in the unfolding drama between proponents of change and defenders of continuity. Taken together, the documents can generate a defensible thesis making a claim that ideas about natural rights escalated a dispute over taxation into a demand for independence.

STRATEGY 4
OPEN WITH A DBQ TWO-STEP

There are times when a combo opening paragraph may not work. Don't worry! The DBQ Two-Step provides a second acceptable option. Simply begin by writing an opening paragraph that presents your thesis statement. This short paragraph will probably be 2 to 3 sentences long. Then write a second paragraph that presents the context or historical setting for your DBQ's topic.

STRATEGY 5
CRAFT A SOPHISTICATED THESIS

A sophisticated thesis is one of the hallmarks of a top scoring DBQ essay. A sophisticated thesis establishes a defensible and nuanced line of reasoning. A nuance is a shade of difference. For example, if a DBQ prompt asks for "the extent of change" a sophisticated thesis would acknowledge the existence of BOTH change and continuity. Similarly, if the DBQ prompt asks for "the causes" or "the effects" of a historic development, a sophisticated thesis would identify BOTH the presence of multiple causes and multiple effects.

A sophisticated thesis requires you to make a judgment and then incorporate that judgment into your thesis. For example, how extensive was the change in ideas about American independence during the years between 1763 and 1776? A standard one-dimensional thesis would assert that a growing commitment to republican values caused many colonists to accuse the British government of violating their natural rights and to support a movement for self-government. You can create a sophisticated thesis by adding this sentence: Although some colonists remained loyal to the Crown, in the end a determined group of Patriots overcame their opposition and declared independence from Great Britain. The transitional phrases "although" and "in the end" create a nuanced line of reasoning.

It is important to note that a standard one-dimensional thesis and a sophisticated thesis will both earn one rubric point. So what is the advantage of crafting a sophisticated thesis? A sophisticated thesis will play a crucial role in helping you establish a nuanced line of reasoning that will enable your essay to earn the complexity point. It thus establishes your essay as a strong candidate to earn a high score.

STRATEGY 6
PLOW THRU AND/OR GROUP

The 2023 APUSH scoring rubric awards 1 point for an essay that uses the contents of at least three documents to address the topic of the prompt. However, the rubric awards 2 points for an essay that uses six documents to support an argument in response to the prompt. What is the most efficient organizational strategy to earn these points?

Many students use an organizational strategy known as "plowing thru." Plowing thru means selecting six documents and then devoting a separate paragraph to each of these documents. This can be a very efficient strategy for earning rubric points. Consider using the "plowing thru" strategy if you feel uncomfortable with the prompt and if the documents do not fall into obvious categories.

Although plowing thru can be an efficient strategy, most teachers have always encouraged students to group the documents into similar conceptual categories. For example, Documents 2 and 4 in our sample DBQ both illustrate the growing importance of republican ideals. At the same time, Documents 3 and 6 illustrate the growth of dissident voices alarmed by the escalating violence unleashed by the revolutionary fervor. Grouping documents demonstrates a high level of insight and analysis that can earn the complexity point.

Plowing thru and grouping are not mutually exclusive strategies. The seven documents will rarely fall into two or three compact categories. Given this situation, the most realistic strategy is to devote some paragraphs to a single document while devoting others to two or more documents.

STRATEGY 7
USE HAPPY TO EARN A SOURCING POINT

The 2023 APUSH scoring rubric awards 1 point for sourcing or explaining how or why a document's historical setting, intended audience, point of view, OR purpose is relevant to your thesis. These four criteria form the easily remembered acronym HAPPY. The H stands for Historical setting, the A stands for Audience, the first P stands for Point of view, and the second P stands for Purpose. And finally, the Y reminds you to apply one of these criteria to a document and then explain Y it is important.

Here are examples of using HAPPY to source four of the documents in our sample DBQ:

Historic setting:
Document 3 is related to the Boston Massacre and other escalating acts of violence. This helps prove that some influential colonists warned that the will of the people is not always constructive.

Audience:
Document 2 was intended to be read by other colonial assemblies. This helps prove the growing commitment to republican ideas.

Point of View:
The author of Document 7 fully endorses the idea of American independence. This helps demonstrate the dramatic shift from colonists loyal to a monarch ruling by divine right to an independent people committed to the republican idea of self-government.

Purpose:
The purpose of Document 1 is to persuade Parliament to enact a Stamp Act to raise revenue. This promoted the Virginia House of Burgesses to challenge Parliament's authority to tax the colonists.

STRATEGY 8
OUTSIDE EVIDENCE

The 2023 APUSH scoring rubric awards 1 point for an example of evidence beyond that which is found in your seven DBQ documents. Outside evidence includes pertinent events, developments, and ideas that are not directly discussed in your seven documents. Well selected outside evidence adds depth and insight to your argument.

Each of your seven documents can be used as a cue that will help you recall outside information you can weave into your essay. For example, the author of Document 4 tells us he is alarmed by "lawless mobs and riots." What events do you think he is referring to? The Boston Massacre would qualify as a relevant example of outside evidence. In contrast, Shays's Rebellion would not qualify because it is outside the chronological boundaries of your prompt.

STRATEGY 9
THREE STEPS TO COMPLEXITY

The complexity point is by far the most difficult part of the 2023 DBQ scoring rubric. Readers will award this point to less than 5 percent of all APUSH essays. It is very important to remember that complexity is only worth one point. You can easily earn an overall score of 5 without it.

According to the 2023 APUSH rubric, complexity means demonstrating an insightful and nuanced understanding of the historical development that is the focus of the prompt. You can demonstrate complexity by incorporating three key features into your essay. First and foremost, write a sophisticated thesis that explains BOTH change and continuity or BOTH multiple causes and effects. Second, let your documents "talk to each other." For example, in Document 7 John Adams dismisses Loyalists, like the author of Document 5, as 'well-meaning, though weak and mistaken people." And finally, write a succinct concluding paragraph that summarizes your argument.

STRATEGY 10
ADD A CONCLUSION

The DBQ scoring rubric does not require a conclusion. However, many readers recommend that students add a concluding paragraph. They report that students often write a more focused thesis in their conclusions than the preliminary one in their opening paragraph. A concise conclusion thus provides readers with a restated thesis that ties your essay together.

CHAPTER 3
ANNOTATED SAMPLE ESSAY

Practice is the key to performing well on the DBQ. This chapter reprints the same DBQ from Chapter 2. It then provides an annotated sample essay that serves as a model of a Level 7 essay. The essay employs the strategies discussed in Chapter 2.

PROMPT

Evaluate the extent of change in ideas about American independence from 1763 to 1776.

DOCUMENT 1

Source: British Order in Council, 1763.

We, the Commissioners of your Majesty's Treasury, beg leave humbly to represent to your Majesty that having taken into consideration the present state of the duties of customs imposed on your Majesty's subjects in America and the West Indies, we find that the revenue arising therefrom is very small and inconsiderable,...and is not yet sufficient to defray a fourth part of the expense necessary for collecting it. We observe with concern that through neglect, connivance, and fraud, not only is revenue impaired, but the commerce of the colonies diverted from its natural course...[This revenue] is more indispensable when the military establishment necessary for maintaining these colonies requires a large revenue to support it, and when their vast increase in territory and population makes the proper regulation of their trade of immediate necessity.

DOCUMENT 2

Source: The Virginia House of Burgesses, The Virginia Resolutions on the Stamp Act, 1765.

Resolved, that the taxation of the people by themselves, or by persons chosen by themselves to represent them, who can only know what taxes the people are able to bear, or the easiest method of raising them, and must themselves be affected by every tax laid on the people, is the only security against burdensome taxation, and the distinguishing characteristic of British freedom, without which the ancient constitution cannot exist.

Resolved, that his Majesty's liege people of this ancient colony have enjoyed the right of being thus governed by their own Assembly in the article of taxes and internal police, and that the same have never been forfeited, or any other way yielded up, but have been constantly recognized by the king and people of Great Britain.

DOCUMENT 3

Source: Mather Byles, renowned Boston Loyalist minister, question posed March 1770.

They call me a brainless Tory; but tell me, my young friend: Which is better – to be ruled by one tyrant three thousand miles away or by three thousand tyrants not a mile away?

DOCUMENT 4

Source: Samuel Adams, The Rights of the Colonists, 1772.

All men have a right to remain in a state of nature as long as they please; and in case of intolerable oppression, civil or religious, to leave the society they belong to, and enter into another. When men enter into society, it is by voluntary consent; and they have a right to demand and insist upon the performance of such conditions and previous limitations as form an equitable original compact…

The natural liberty of man is to be free from any superior power on earth, and not to be under the will or legislative authority of man, but only to have the law of nature for his rule.

DOCUMENT 5

Source: Joseph Galloway, "A Plan of a Proposed Union Between Great Britain and the Colonies", proposal debated and then rejected by the First Continental Congress, 1774.

That a British and American legislature, for regulating the administration of the general affairs of America, be proposed and established in America., including all the said colonies; within, and under which government, each colony shall retain its present constitution, and powers of regulating and governing its own internal police, in all cases whatsoever.

That the said government be administered by a President General, to be appointed by the King and a Grand Council, to be chosen by the representatives of the people of the several colonies, in their respective assemblies, once in every three years.

DOCUMENT 6

Source: In "Plain English," a Loyalist describes the reign of "lawless mobs," 1775.

Some of these people, who from a sense of their duty to the king, and a reverence for his laws, have behaved quietly and peaceably; and for which reason they have been deprived of their liberty, abused in their persons, and suffered such barbarous cruelties, insults, and indignities, besides the loss of their property, by the hands of lawless mobs and riots, as would have been disgraceful even for savages to have committed. The courts of justice being shut up in most parts of the province [Massachusetts], and the justices of those courts compelled by armed force, headed by some of your Congress, to refrain from doing their duties, at present it is rendered impracticable for those sufferers to obtain redress…

DOCUMENT 7

Source: John Adams, Letters of John Adams, Addressed to his Wife, July 3, 1776

The hopes of reconciliation, which were fondly entertained by multitudes of honest and well meaning, though weak and mistaken people, have been gradually and, at last, totally extinguished. Time has been given for the whole people maturely to consider the great question of independence, and to ripen their judgment, dissipate their fears, and allure their hopes, by discussing it in newspapers and pamphlets, by debating it in assemblies, conventions, committees of safety and inspection, in town and county meetings, as well as in private conversations, so that the whole people, in every colony of the thirteen, have now adopted it as their own act....

I am well aware of the toil, and blood, and treasure, that it will cost us to maintain this Declaration, and support and defend these States. Yes, through all the gloom, I can see the rays of ravishing light and glory. I can see that the end is more than worth all the means. And that posterity will triumph in that day's transaction.

SAMPLE ANNOTATED ESSAY

In 1763, the British and their American colonists celebrated a glorious victory in the French and Indian War. While the Americans rejoiced and looked forward to enjoying a new era of peace and prosperity, somber British finance ministers faced an enormous national debt. The crisis forced the British government to shift its economic policies by ending the period of salutary neglect, enforcing the Navigation Acts, and enacting new taxes to raise revenue. The change in British economic policies began the process of straining long-standing ties between the North American colonies and their mother country. A growing commitment to the ideas of republican government caused many colonists to accuse the British government of violating their natural rights. Although some colonists remained loyal to the Crown, in the end a determined group of Patriots overcame their opposition and embraced the idea of independence.

Britain's financial crisis prompted the Commissioners of the King's Treasury to evaluate the empire's trade and taxation policies (Doc 1). The Commissioners discovered that revenue from customs duties was "very small and inconsiderable." The purpose of Document 1 was to persuade King George III and his first minister George Grenville to end the period of salutary neglect by enacting a Stamp Act to raise revenue from the North American colonies.

Contextualization: Useful background information relates the topic of the prompt to broader historic events in 1763.

Thesis: The thesis makes a clear defensible claim that establishes a nuanced line of reasoning.

Document 1 is accurately described and used as evidence to support the thesis argument.

The discussion presents a valid Purpose analysis for Document 1.

The Stamp Act raised questions about Parliament's right to tax the colonists. In 1765, the Virginia House of Burgesses passed a series of Resolutions on the Stamp Act (Doc 2). The resolutions directly challenged Parliament's authority to tax the colonies. While continuing to express loyalty to the king, the Resolutions insisted that local control over taxation represented a "distinguishing characteristic of British freedom." As intended by the House of Burgesses, copies of the Virginia Resolutions were quickly distributed to other colonial assemblies. The Resolutions thus mobilized public opposition to the Stamp Act while at the same time beginning the process of a shift in public opinion from allegiance to the king to support for new ideas about the need for American independence.

Document 2 is accurately described and used as evidence to support the thesis argument.

The discussion presents a valid Purpose analysis for Document 2.

The economic dispute over taxes quickly ignited a political movement inspired by republican values. Republicanism is the belief that government should be based upon the consent of the governed. The trans-Atlantic exchange of Enlightenment ideas familiarized Samuel Adams and other colonial leaders with John Locke's theory of natural rights. In "The Rights of the Colonists" (Doc 4), Adams asserted that "the natural liberty of man is to be free from any superior power on earth." Adams thus turned to Enlightenment ideas of natural rights to undermine the existing belief in the divine right of kings. This marked an important change from accepting the divine right of a distant ruler to a system based upon the will of the people.

The trans-Atlantic exchange of Enlightenment ideas is presented as relevant Outside Information.

Document 4 is accurately described and used as evidence to support the thesis argument.

The growing calls for independence alarmed Loyalists who valued tradition, law and order, and allegiance to the Crown. They pointed to escalating acts of violence such as the Boston Massacre and the Boston Tea Party as examples of the actions of lawless mobs that proclaimed liberty for themselves while denying it to liberty for themselves while denying it to others. In Doc 6 a Loyalist decries the "barbarous cruelties, insults, and indignities" inflicted on peaceful citizens. The violence in Boston distressed Mather Byles, In Doc 3 Byles poses as a "brainless Tory," who asks why the rule of one tyrant reigning three thousand miles across the Atlantic Ocean is worse than the rule of "three thousand tyrants not a mile away." His insightful question was intended to challenge the republican assumption that the will of the people will always be constructive.

The Boston Massacre and the Boston Tea Party are presented as relevant <u>Outside Information</u>.

Document 3 is accurately described and used as evidence to support the thesis argument.

The discussion presents a valid <u>Purpose</u> analysis for Document 3.

Byles's question underscored the possible dangers posed by the shifting ideas about American independence. Moderates tried to find a compromise between submission to British authority and the unknown perils of independence. Like other Loyalists, Joseph Galloway (Doc 5) proposed a plan intended to resolve the crisis by creating an "American legislature" responsible for the "general affairs of America." However, the First Continental Congress narrowly defeated Galloway's plan.

Document 5 is accurately described as evidence to support the thesis argument.

The discussion presents a valid <u>Purpose</u> analysis for Document 5.

As 1776 opened, popular sentiment vacillated between calls for independence and pleas for compromise. However, the publication of *Common Sense* by Thomas Paine caused a dramatic change in public support for independence. Paine rejected monarchy and attacked King George III as a "royal brute." He urged Americans to create an independent nation based upon republican principles.

The discussion of *Common Sense* is presented as relevant <u>Outside Information</u>.

Paine's compelling arguments emboldened John Adams. In Doc 7, Adams dismisses Loyalists such as Joseph Galloway (Doc 5) as "honest and well-meaning, though weak and mistaken people." He proudly notes that the "whole people" had considered and approved "the grand question of independence." Although aware the struggle for independence would require great sacrifice, Adams confidently predicted that the reward of freedom would be more than worth the cost.

Document 7 is accurately described as evidence to support the thesis argument.

The Patriots overcame the objections of Loyalists and issued the Declaration of Independence the day after Adams penned Doc 7. The Declaration of Independence documented a historic shift in ideas about American independence. Colonists once loyal to a king now committed themselves to the republican idea of self-rule.

A concise conclusion restates the nuanced thesis.

SCORING SUMMARY

CONTEXTUALIZATION	1 point	Sentences 1 - 4 establish the relevant historic context.
THESIS	1 point	Sentences 5 – 6 provide a sophisticated and nuanced thesis.
DOCUMENT CONTENT	2 points	The content of six documents is used to support the thesis.
EVIDENCE BEYOND THE DOCUMENTS	1 point	Locke's theory of natural rights is relevant to Document 4. The Boston Massacre and the Boston Tea Party are relevant to Documents 3 and 6. *Common Sense* is relevant to Document 7.
ANALYSIS (HAPPY)	1 point	Essay identifies the purpose of Documents 1, 2, 3, and 5.
COMPLEXITY	1 point	Essay begins with a sophisticated and nuanced thesis. Documents 2 and 4 and 5 and 4 talk to each other. Concluding paragraph summarizes the thesis argument.
	7 points	

UNIT II
CONTINUITY AND CHANGE

CHAPTER 4
INTRODUCING CONTINUITY AND CHANGE

The historical processes of continuity and change are all around us. For example, the automobile industry floods the country with advertisements touting their new models every autumn. Although the new cars do include visible changes, the cars remain fundamentally the same. Automobiles have been undergoing the twin processes of continuity and change since "horseless carriages" first appeared in the 1890s.

A knowledge of continuity and change helps history students answer the question, "How did we get to this point?" These processes can also provide clues to answering the question, "Where do we go from here?"

The College Board recognizes the important roles continuity and change play in the chain of developments that comprise the American experience. APUSH exam writers expect students to demonstrate an ability to recognize, analyze, and evaluate the dynamic processes of continuity and change.

RECOGNIZING A CONTINUITY AND CHANGE DBQ PROMPT

The historical processes of continuity and change play particularly important roles in DBQ questions. During the past few years well over half of all DBQ prompts have asked students to demonstrate their ability to use this historical thinking skill. Here are three examples:

1. Evaluate the extent of change in American foreign policy from 1919 to 1939.

2. Evaluate the extent of change in American culture during the period from 1945 to 1963.

3. Evaluate the extent of continuity and change in the lives of American women from 1940 to 1975.

Note that DBQ prompts typically use the phrase "evaluate the extent of" to introduce a continuity and change prompt.

CREATING AN ORGANIZATIONAL CHART

The College Board recommends that you spend about 15 minutes reading and analyzing the seven DBQ documents. Many students find it helpful to create a chart to help them organize their thoughts and keep track of the documents. The sample chart below contains columns for Sources, Continuity, Change, and HAPPY Analysis.

Writing a DBQ essay requires great concentration. Given the time pressure, it is easy to lose track of the documents and the key point you want to make. An organizational chart can serve as a valuable reference as you write your DBQ essay.

	Sources	Continuity	Change	HAPPY Analysis
Document 1				
Document 2				
Document 3				
Document 4				
Document 5				
Document 6				
Document 7				

CHAPTER 5

SLAVERY IN THE SOUTH
1800 - 1850

PROMPT

Evaluate the extent of continuity and change in the lives of enslaved Africans in the South during the period 1800 to 1850.

DOCUMENT 1

Source: William Lloyd Garrison, "Declaration of Sentiments of the American Anti-Slavery Society," 1833.

With entire confidence in the overruling justice of God, we plant ourselves upon the Declaration of Independence, and upon the truths of Divine Revelation....

We shall organize Anti-Slavery Societies, if possible, in every city, town, and village of our land...

We will do all that in us lies consistently with this Declaration of our principles, to overthrow the most execrable system of slavery that has ever been witnessed upon earth; to deliver our land from its deadliest curse; to wipe out the foulest stain which rests upon our nation; and to secure to the colored population of the United States, all the rights and privileges which belong to them as men, and as Americans – come what may to our persons, our interests, or our reputations – whether we live to witness the triumph of Justice, Liberty and Humanity, or perish untimely as martyrs in this great, benevolent, and holy cause.

DOCUMENT 2

Source: Bennet H. Barrow, wealthy Louisiana planter, "Rules of Highland Plantation," 1838.

No Negro shall leave the place at any time without my permission... No Negro shall be allowed to marry out of the plantation. No Negro shall be allowed to sell anything without my express permission. I have ever maintained the doctrine that my Negroes have no time whatever, that they are always liable to my call without questioning for a moment the propriety, of it. I adhere to this on the grounds of expedience and right. The very security of the plantation requires that a general and uniform control over the people of it should be exercised...To render this part of the rule justly applicable, however, it would be necessary that such a settled arrangement should exist on the plantation to make it unnecessary for a Negro to leave it – or to have a good plea for doing so. You must therefore make him as comfortable at home as possible, affording him what is essentially necessary for his happiness – you must provide for him yourself and by that means create in him a habit of perfect dependence on you.

DOCUMENT 3

Source: Sarah T. Smith, Speech at the Second Anti-Slavery Convention of American Women held in Philadelphia, 1838.

We are told that it is not within the "province of woman," to discuss the subject of slavery; that it is a "political question," and we are "stepping out of our sphere," when we take part in its discussion. It is not true that it is merely a political question, it is likewise a question of justice, of humanity, of morality, of religion; a question which, while it involves considerations of immense importance to the welfare and prosperity of our country, enters deeply into the home-concerns, the every-day feelings of millions of our fellow beings. Whether the laborer shall receive the reward of his labor, or be driven daily to unrequited toil...whether his bones and sinews shall be his own, or another's; whether his child shall receive the protection of its natural guardian, or be ranked among the livestock of the estate, to be disposed of as the caprice or interest of the master may dictate – these considerations are all involved in the question of liberty or slavery.

DOCUMENT 4

Source: John C. Calhoun, political leader from South Carolina, 1844

The condition of the African race throughout all the States where the ancient relation between the two races has been retained enjoys a degree of health and comfort which may well compare with that of the laboring population of any country in Christendom; and, it may be added that in no other condition, or in any other age or country, has the Negro race ever attained so high an elevation in morals, intelligence, or civilization.

DOCUMENT 5

Source: Frederick Douglass, *Narrative of the Life of Frederick Douglass, An American Slave, Written by Himself*, 1845

If at any one time of my life more than another, I was made to drink the bitterest dregs of slavery, that time was during the first six months of my stay with Mr. Covey [a White overseer]…Mr. Covey succeeded in breaking me. I was broken in body, soul, and spirit. My natural elasticity was crushed, my intellect languished, the disposition to read departed, the cheerful spark that lingered about my eye died; the dark night of slavery closed in upon me; and behold a man transformed me into a brute!

DOCUMENT 6

Source: Harriet Jacobs, *Incidents in the Life of a Slave Girl*, published in 1861

I turned from him with disgust and hatred. But he was my master. I was compelled to live under the same roof with him – where I saw a man forty years my senior daily violating the most sacred commandment of nature. He told me I was his property; that I must be subject to his will in all things. My soul revolted against the mean tyranny. But where could I turn for protection? No matter whether the slave girl be as black as ebony or as fair as her mistress. In either case, there is no shadow of law to protect her from insult, from violence, or even from death; all these are inflicted by fiends who bear the shape of men. The mistress, who ought to protect the helpless victim, has no other feelings towards her but those of jealousy and rage…

DOCUMENT 7

Source: Historical Statistics of the United States, 1970

POPULATION OF THE SOUTH, 1790 – 1850

Year	White	Freed Slaves	Slaves
1790	1,240,454	32,523	654,121
1800	1,691,892	61,575	851,532
1810	2,118144	97,284	1,103,700
1820	2,867,454	130,487	1,509,904
1830	3,614,600	175,074	1,983,860
1840	4,601,873	207,214	2,481,390
1850	6,184,477	235,821	3,200,364

ORGANIZATIONAL CHART

	Sources	Continuity	Change	HAPPY Analysis
Document 1	Abolitionist leader		Strongly opposes slavery	Purpose
Document 2	Southern slaveholder	Rules to regulate slavery		Purpose
Document 3	Female abolitionist		Calls upon women to join abolitionist crusade	Purpose
Document 4	Prominent defender of slavery	Slavery is a "positive good"		Point of view
Document 5	Prominent former slave		Leading black abolitionist	Historic situation
Document 6	Prominent former slave	Abuse of enslaved women		Point of view
Document 7	Government statistics	Population of slaves steadily increases	Population of freed slaves gradually increases	

SAMPLE ANNOTATED ESSAY

In 1790, the once vibrant Southern economy began to stagnate as tobacco lost its value as a cash crop. However, the invention of the cotton gin in 1793 revolutionized the Southern economy and the lives of enslaved Africans. As the South became committed to a one-crop economy it also became committed to slavery. The period between 1800 and 1850 witnessed both changes and enduring continuities in the lives of enslaved Africans living in the South. The rise of an active abolitionist movement in the North and a gradual increase in the number of freed slaves did represent important changes. Although significant, in the end these changes did not alter the basic continuity that slavery remained a growing, immoral, and race-based system of perpetual bondage.

Contextualization: Useful background information relates the topic of the prompt to broader events in 1800.

Thesis: The thesis makes a clear defensible claim that establishes a nuanced line of reasoning.

During the late 1700s and early 1800s, many Southern leaders referred to slavery as a "necessary evil" inherited from their colonial past. However, as the South's cotton-based economy became more profitable, slaveholders like John C. Calhoun (Document 4) and Bennet Barrow (Document 2) defended slavery as a "positive good." As a slaveholder, former vice-president and senator from South Carolina, Calhoun emerged as one of the South's most influential defenders of slavery. In Document 4 Calhoun expressed the point of view of Southern planters that their slaves enjoyed lives that compared favorably with "the laboring population of any country in Christendom." In Document 2, Barrow adds another perspective on Calhoun's "positive good" argument. Written as advice for other planters, Barrow recommends strict rules to maintain plantation discipline and the "habit of

Documents 2 and 4 are accurately described and used as evidence to support the thesis argument.

The discussion presents a valid Point of View analysis for Document 4.

The discussion presents a valid Purpose analysis for Document 2.

of perfect dependence." However, Barrow's reference to "security" reveals his underlying insecurity and fear of possible resistance.

Slavery became an entrenched part of the South's economy and way of life. Although most Americans accepted slavery, William Lloyd Garrison did not. Garrison was a young reformer influenced by the Second Great Awakening's belief in perfectionism – faith in the human ability to build a just society. At first, he supported the American Colonization Society's plan to return freed slaves to Africa. However, his contact with slavery in Baltimore convinced Garrison that slavery was cruel and immoral. He rejected the American Colonization Society's gradual approach and co-founded the American Anti-Slavery Society. In Document 1, he calls slavery a "foul stain" that contradicts the Declaration of Independence and "the overruling justice of God." Garrison's harsh language underscored his determination to directly challenge the "positive good" argument advanced by Calhoun (Doc 4) and other defenders of slavery.

The discussion of Garrison's personal story is presented as relevant Outside Information.

The discussion presents a valid Purpose analysis for Document 1.

Garrison's denunciation of slavery as a moral outrage inspired Northern women to join the abolitionist movement. In Document 3, Sarah T. Smith addressed the Second Anti-Slavery Convention of American Women held in Philadelphia. Smith's speech had two purposes. First, to refute the widespread belief that slavery was a "political question" that women should not be allowed to discuss in public. And second, to convince her listeners that slavery was a "question of justice, of humanity, of morality" that affected all Americans. Like Garrison, Smith did not see slavery as an issue that could be compromised.

The discussion presents a valid Purpose analysis for Document 3.

Garrison's call for the immediate abolition of slavery promised a possible change in the lives of enslaved Africans. However, the abolition movement had little direct impact upon the vast majority of enslaved Africans. Documents 5 and 6 provide descriptions of the underlying continuity of slavery in the South. Harriet Jacob's alarming description in Document 6 provides compelling evidence that the law did not protect slaves. Her account also demonstrates a significant gap between the professed ideal of the cult of domesticity and the realities of a slave woman's life. In Document 5, Frederick Douglass vividly describes how slavery crushed his spirit and turned him "into a brute." He ultimately escaped and became one of the foremost antislavery activists. This vivid passage from his famous autobiography helped mobilize opposition to slavery.

The writings of Garrison, Smith, Douglass and Jacobs suggest the possibility of changes in the South's "peculiar institution." The table in Document 7 does document a steady rise in the number of free nonwhites. However, these figures are dwarfed by the surging population of slaves. As a result, continuity remained the dominant factor in the lives of enslaved Africans living in the South.

Documents 5 and 6 are accurately described and used as evidence to support the thesis argument.

The discussion presents a valid Point of View analysis for Document 6.

The discussion presents a valid Historic Situation analysis for Document 5.

Document 7 is accurately described and used as evidence to support the thesis argument.

COMMENTARY

This model essay would receive all 7 rubric points. A sophisticated thesis in paragraph 1 establishes a nuanced line of reasoning. The essay skillfully groups documents into paragraphs that encourage insightful comparisons. The concluding paragraph provides a brief but effective restatement of the thesis.

SCORING SUMMARY

CONTEXTUALIZATION	1 point	The first three sentences establish the relevant historic setting.
THESIS	1 point	Sentences 4 - 6 provide a sophisticated thesis that establishes a nuanced approach to both change and continuity.
DOCUMENT CONTENT	2 points	The essay uses all seven documents to support the thesis.
EVIDENCE BEYOND THE DOCUMENTS	1 point	The discussions of the Second Great Awakening and the American Colonization Society in paragraph 3 provide relevant background information that explain Garrison's motivation. Paragraph 4 uses the cult of domesticity as outside evidence to underscore the significance of Jacob's account.
ANALYSIS (HAPPY)	1 point	The essay identifies the purpose of documents 1, 2, and 3; the point of view of Documents 4 and 6; and the historic situation for Document 5.
COMPLEXITY	1 point	The essay begins with a sophisticated thesis that addresses both continuity and change. It uses grouping to provide organization and insight. The concluding paragraph restates the thesis.
	7 points	

CHAPTER 6
AFRICAN AMERICANS IN THE SOUTH 1865 – 1900

PROMPT

Evaluate the extent of change and continuity in the lives of African Americans in the South during the period 1865 to 1900.

DOCUMENT 1

Source: Carl Schurz, *Report on the Condition of the South*, 1865

There is, at present, no danger of another insurrection against the authority of the United States on a large scale, and the people are willing to reconstruct their State governments, and to send their senators and representatives to Congress. But as to the moral value of these results, we must not indulge in any delusions …. There is, as yet, among the Southern people an utter absence of national feeling…

Aside from the assumption that the Negro will not work without physical compulsion, there appears to be another popular notion… that the Negro exists for the special object of raising cotton, rice, and sugar for the whites, and that it is illegitimate for him to indulge, like other people, in the pursuit of his own happiness in his own way.

DOCUMENT 2

Source: Laws of St. Landry Parish, Louisiana, 1865

No Negro shall be allowed to pass within the limits of said parish without special permit in writing from his employer.

Every Negro is required to be in the regular service of some white person, or former owner, who shall be held responsible for the conduct of said Negro.

No public meeting or congregations of Negroes shall be allowed within said parish after sunset…

No Negro shall be permitted to preach, exhort, or otherwise declaim to congregations of colored people, without special permission in writing from the president of the police jury…

No Negro who is not in the military service shall be allowed to carry firearms, or any kind of weapons, within the parish, without the special written permission of his employer…

It shall be the duty of every citizen to act as a police officer for the detection of offenses and the apprehension of offenders, who shall be immediately handed over to the proper captain or chief of patrol.

DOCUMENT 3

Source: Interview with Henry Blake, African American farmer in Little Rock Arkansas, as part of the Federal Writers' Project, a government program during the Great Depression.

After freedom, we worked on shares a while…When we worked on shares, we couldn't make nothing, just overalls and something to eat. Half went to the other man and you would destroy your half if you weren't careful. A man that didn't know how to count would always lose. He might lose anyhow. They didn't give no itemized statement. No, you just had to take their word. They never gave you no details. They just say you owe so much. No matter how good account you kept, you had to go by their account…They'd keep you in debt… Anything that kept you a slave because he was always right and you were always wrong if there was a difference.

DOCUMENT 4

Source: Fifteenth Amendment to the United States Constitution, 1870

Section 1. The right of citizens of the United States to vote shall not be denied or abridged by the United States or by any state on account of race, color, or previous condition of servitude.

Section 2. The Congress shall have power to enforce this article by appropriate legislation.

DOCUMENT 5

Thomas Nast in *Harper's Weekly*, October 24, 1874, Library of Congress

DOCUMENT 6

Source: Booker T. Washington, "Atlanta Compromise Address",
September 11, 1895

We have proved our loyalty to you in the past, in nursing your children, watching by the sickbed of your mothers and fathers, and often following them with tear-dimmed eyes to their graves, so in the future, in our humble way, we shall stand by you with devotion that no foreigner can approach, ready to lay down our lives, if need be, in defense of yours, interlacing our industrial, commercial, civil, and religious life with yours in a way that shall make the interests of both races one. In all things that are purely social we can be as separate as the fingers, yet one as the hand in all things essential to mutual progress.... The wisest among my race understand that the agitation of questions of social equality is the extremist folly, and that progress in the enjoyment of all the privileges that will come to us must be the result of severe and constant struggle rather than of artificial forcing...The opportunity to earn a dollar in a factory just now is worth infinitely more than the opportunity to spend a dollar in an opera house.

DOCUMENT 7

Source: William A. Sinclair, historian and former slave, *The Aftermath of Slavery*,
1905

Schools were planted: the lower grades; the preparatory schools; the normal schools; the colleges; the professional schools....For a time this work of education was supported by the National Government, supplemented by Northern benevolence and by a nominal fee which was charged the colored parent for each child...As a result of this impetus the colored man can make this showing in a single generation:

Educationally his illiteracy has been cut down forty-seven percent, although there are nearly three times as many colored people today as were emancipated. He fills the common schools with 1,200,000 of his children; 30,000 are in schools for higher learning, and trade schools; over 200 are pursuing studies in Northern universities, or taking special courses in European institutions...It may be noted that 278 colored women are among the graduates of colleges...

ORGANIZATIONAL CHART

	Sources	Continuity	Change	HAPPY Analysis
Document 1	First-person report	Defeated but defiant		Intended audience
Document 2	Legal code	Slavery by another name		Purpose
Document 3	Sharecropper	Cycle of poverty and debt		Point of view
Document 4	Constitutional amendment		Enfranchise black voters	Purpose
Document 5	Political cartoon	Dramatize Klan violence		Point of view
Document 6	Public address	Advocate black self-help and accomodation		Purpose/ Intended audience
Document 7	Historical report		Public education for African Americans	Purpose

SAMPLE ANNOTATED ESSAY

The end of the Civil War presented the newly freed slaves with many challenges. During the period from 1865 to 1900, African Americans experienced both change and continuity. The Fifteenth Amendment enfranchised black voters while new schools provided black children with unprecedented educational opportunities. Although these changes marked significant advances, in the end a combination of legal discrimination, sharecropping and Klan violence imposed a repressive system of white supremacy that represented continuity with the South's past history of subordinating African Americans.

Thesis: The thesis makes a defensible claim that establishes a nuanced line of reasoning.

The aftermath of the Civil War ushered in a period of great uncertainty. The defeated and embittered Southern states faced difficult questions about the future place of over four million freedmen. Lincoln's generously promised "malice toward none, with charity for all." But his tragic assassination left the nation with an untested new president whose support for white supremacy openly clashed with the Radical Republicans in Congress.

Contextualization: Useful background information relates the topic of the prompt to broader events at the end of the Civil War.

Slavery's long legacy of prejudice and discrimination could not be easily overcome. In a report (Document 1) delivered to Congress, Carl Schurz confirmed that there was "no danger of another insurrection." However, he also reported that Southern attitudes toward their former slaves had not changed. Whites uniformly opposed reforms that would grant civil rights to the freedmen. Instead, they sought to create a system as close to slavery as possible. Newly enacted Black Codes strongly supported Schurz's

Documents 1 and 2 are accurately described and used as evidence to support the thesis argument.

pessimistic conclusion. Document 2 provides examples from a Black Code adopted in St. Landry Parish, Louisiana. The white lawmakers designed the code to preserve a social, economic, and legal system that resembled slavery in everything but name. For example, the code barred black people from speaking in public, owning firearms, or moving freely within the parish.

The discussion presents a valid Intended Audience analysis for Document 1.

The discussion presents a valid Purpose analysis for Document 2.

Although the Civil War freed the slaves, it did not bring them economic prosperity. During the late 1860s cotton planters and black freedmen entered sharecropping agreements. In this system, black families exchanged their labor for the use of a planter's land, tools, and seed. In Document 3 a former sharecropper named Henry Blake recounts the difficulties he faced dealing with unscrupulous merchants and planters. Blake poignantly notes that, "a man that didn't know how to count would always lose." His point of view is clear – sharecropping trapped African American farmers in a seemingly endless cycle of poverty and debt that showed strong continuity with slavery.

Document 3 is accurately described and used as evidence to support the thesis argument.

The discussion presents a valid Point of View analysis for Document 3.

Radical Republicans recognized that two centuries of slavery created deeply entrenched racial prejudices that could not be easily changed. Congress passed the Fifteenth Amendment (Document 4) to enable African Americans to exercise political influence for the first time. The newly enfranchised freedmen elected 14 black men to the House of Representatives, two to the Senate, and several hundred to state legislatures. Black voters supported the Republican Party by casting ballots that helped elect Grant in 1868 and 1872.

Document 4 is accurately described and used as evidence to support the thesis argument.

The discussion presents a valid Purpose analysis for Document 4.

The alliance between African Americans and their Republican allies helped bring the Republican Party to power throughout the South. The Republican state legislatures made impressive progress founding the South's first system of state-funded public schools. The author of Document 7 proudly presents impressive statistical evidence to substantiate how African Americans have taken advantage of their new educational opportunities. This progress also led to the founding of a number of black colleges including Howard in Washington, D.C., Morehouse and Spelman in Atlanta, and Fisk in Nashville. These historically black colleges later played a crucial role in training black leaders who led the fight against segregation.

Document 7 is accurately described and used as evidence to support the thesis argument.

The discussion presents a valid Purpose analysis for Document 7.

The discussion of black colleges is presented as relevant Outside Information.

White Southerners continued to believe that vindictive Republicans sought to punish them by repealing Black Codes, enfranchising African Americans, and opening schools for black children. The years following the Civil War witnessed the proliferation of white supremacist organizations. In Document 5 Thomas Nast used a compelling visual image to express his point of view that the newly freed African Americans faced levels of violence that were even worse than in slavery. He portrayed a smiling Klansman and an armed member of a "White League" congratulating each other over an image of black parents mourning the death of their child. The background images underscore rampant violence as a school burns and a black man hangs from a tree.

Document 5 is accurately described and used as evidence to support the thesis argument.

The discussion presents a valid Point of View analysis for Document 5.

Booker T. Washington recognized that violence, inequality, and segregation were continuing realities of black life in the South. As the founder of Tuskegee Institute, Washington became a leading spokesman for black economic self-help and vocational training. In his Atlanta Compromise Speech (Document 6), Washington delivered his deliberately conciliatory message that black and white Americans could lead separate social lives while working together for economic progress. Washington's white audience praised his message of accommodation and self-help.

Carl Schurz, Thomas Nast, Henry Blake, and Booker T. Washington all recognized that African Americans faced an unyielding wall of racism and discrimination. The Supreme Court decision in Plessy v. Ferguson sanctioned these continuities in black life by applying its "separate but equal" doctrine to public facilities.

Document 6 is accurately described and used as evidence to support the thesis argument.

The discussion presents a valid Purpose analysis for Document 6.

A concise conclusion restates the thesis.

COMMENTARY

This model essay would receive all 7 rubric points. Paragraph 1 presents a sophisticated thesis that establishes a nuanced line of reasoning. Paragraph 2 establishes the historic context for understanding the extent of continuity and change in the lives of African Americans in the South following the Civil War. The essay presents Documents 3,4, 5, 6, and 7 in separate paragraphs. However, the essay groups Documents 1 and 2 into a single paragraph. The concluding paragraph provides a brief but effective restatement of the thesis.

SCORING SUMMARY

CONTEXTUALIZATION	1 point	Paragraph 2 establishes the historic context.
THESIS	1 point	Paragraph 1 provides a sophisticated thesis that establishes a nuanced approach to both continuity and change.
DOCUMENT CONTENT	2 points	The essay uses all seven documents to support the thesis.
EVIDENCE BEYOND THE DOCUMENTS	1 point	The discussion of black colleges in paragraph 6 provides relevant outside information.
ANALYSIS (HAPPY)	1 point	The essay identifies the purpose of Documents 2, 4, 6, and 7; the point of view of Documents 3 and 5; and the intended audience for Document 1.
COMPLEXITY	1 point	The essay begins with a sophisticated thesis that addresses both continuity and change. It provides in-depth analysis that includes grouping Documents 1 and 2 The concluding paragraph provides a succinct restatement of the thesis.
	7 points	

CHAPTER 7
THE GREAT MIGRATION
1900 – 1930

PROMPT

Evaluate the extent of continuity and change in the social and economic experiences of African Americans who migrated from the rural South to urban areas in the North in the period 1900 to 1930.

DOCUMENT 1

Source: National Association for the Advancement of Colored People, Founding Statement, May 30, 1909

If Lincoln could revisit this country in the flesh, he would be disheartened and discouraged. He would learn that on January 1, 1909, Georgia had rounded out a new confederacy by disfranchising the Negro, after the manner of all the other Southern states....In many states Lincoln would find justice enforced, if at all, by judges elected by one element of the community to pass upon the liberties and lives of another. He would see the black men and women, whose freedom a hundred thousand soldiers gave their lives, set apart in trains, in which they pay first-class fares for third-class service, and segregated in railway stations and in places of entertainment; he would observe that State after State declines to do its elementary duty in preparing the Negro through education for the best exercise of citizenship.

DOCUMENT 2

Source: Twenty-Sixth Annual Tuskegee Negro Conference Statement, 1917

There is everywhere in the South much unrest because of the opportunities which are being offered our people to go North to work in many industries where there is now a shortage of labor. The Conference would also say: these are transitory times. We recognize and appreciate the opportunities offered in the North to our people and the necessity which is compelling many of them to go there. Right here in the South, however, are great and permanent opportunities for the masses of our people. This section, we feel, is just entering upon its greatest era of development. There are millions of acres of land yet to be cultivated, cities to be built railroads to be extended, hundreds of mines to be worked. Here your labor in the future is going to be in still greater demand.

DOCUMENT 3

Source: U.S. Bureau of the Census, "Populations of the 100 Largest Cities and Other Urban Places in the U.S.: 1790 – 1990."

AFRICAN AMERICANS AS A PERCENTAGE OF THE POPULATION OF SELECTED U.S. CITIES, 1900 – 1950

City	1900	1910	1920	1930	1940	1950
Chicago	1.8	2.0	4.1	6.9	8.2	13.6
Detroit	1.4	1.2	4.1	7.7	9.2	16.2
Los Angelos	2.1	2.4	2.7	3.1	4.2	8.7
New York City	1.8	1.9	2.7	4.7	6.1	9.5
Philadelphia	4.8	5.5	7.4	11.3	13.0	18.2
St. Louis	6.2	6.4	9.0	11.4	13.3	17.9

DOCUMENT 4

Source: Dwight Thompson Farnham, Northern white efficiency expert, article titled "Negroes as a Source of Industrial Labor," Industrial Management, August 1918.

A certain amount of segregation is necessary at times to preserve the peace. This is especially true when Negroes are first introduced into a plant. It is a question if it is not always best to have separate wash rooms and the like. In places where different races necessarily come into close contact and in places where inherited characteristics are especially accentuated, it is better to keep their respective folkways from clashing wherever possible.

DOCUMENT 5

Source: *Chicago Tribune*, description of racial unrest entered in the South Side of Chicago, July 28, 1919

So serious was the trouble throughout the district that the Acting Chief of Police Alcock was unable to place an estimate on the injured. Scores received cuts and bruises from flying stones and rocks but went to their homes for medical attention.

Minor rioting continued through the night all over the South Side. Negroes who were found in the street cars were dragged to the street and beaten. They were first ordered to the street by white men and if they refused the trolley was jerked of the wires,

Scores of conflicts between the whites and blacks were reported at South Side stations and reserves were ordered to stand guard on all important street corners. Some of the fighting took place four miles from the scene of the afternoon riots.

DOCUMENT 6

Source: Marcus Garvey, Declaration of Rights of the Negro Peoples of the World, adopted at the first convention of the Universal Negro Improvement Association (UNIA), August 1920

And now the world is in an upstir! The Universal Negro Improvement Association has succeeded in arousing the sleeping consciousness of millions of Negroes! And that which was thought impossible has now happened. No one thought up to recently that the Negro was capable of striking out of the barriers of racial entanglement to free himself on the great ocean of Truth. This is the age in which truth has a hearing; when men oppressed and men abused are determined that their cause should be heard at the bar of public opinion, and that justice be meted out to them...This is indeed the hour for concentrated action on the part of all of our race...

DOCUMENT 7

Source: Alain LeRoy Locke, *The New Negro*, 1925

If we were to offer a symbol of what Harlem has come to mean in the short span of twenty years it would be another statue of liberty on the landward side of New York. It stands for a folk-movement which in human significance can be compared only with the pushing back of the Western frontier in the first half of the last century, or the waves of immigration which have swept in from overseas in the last half. Numerically, far smaller than either of these movements, the volume of migration is such nonetheless that Harlem has become the greatest Negro community the world has known – without counterpart in the South or in Africa. But beyond this, Harlem represents the Negro's latest thrust toward Democracy...In Harlem, Negro life is seizing upon its first chances for group expression and self-determination.

ORGANIZATIONAL CHART

	Sources	Continuity	Change	HAPPY Analysis
Document 1	NAACP mission statement		Calls for racial justice	Historic Situation
Document 2	Tuskegee message	Stay in the South		Intended Audience
Document 3	US Bureau of the Census		Documents the Great Migration	Purpose
Document 4	White efficiency expert	Limited segregation in the workplace		Intended Audience
Document 5	Newspaper article	Race riot directed at black people living in Chicago		Historic Situation
Document 6	Marcus Garvey		Calls for black pride	Purpose
Document 7	Major Harlem Renaissance writer		Celebrates "New Negro"	Purpose

SAMPLE ANNOTATED ESSAY

During the early 1900s mass movements of people transformed life in American cities. Migrants from American farms and immigrants from villages in Southern and Eastern Europe poured into cities in the Northeast and Midwest. By 1920, the census reported that for the first time a majority of Americans lived in urban areas. As these events unfolded, African Americans began a Great Migration from the rural South to cities in the North. The Great Migration produced both significant changes and continuities in the social, economic, and cultural life of African Americans. Although African Americans living in Northern states continued to experience social and economic discrimination, in the end the cultural concept of the "New Negro" created an enduring change in African American identity.

Contextualization: Useful background information relates the topic of the prompt to broader events in 1900.

Thesis: The thesis makes a clear defensible claim that establishes a nuanced line of reasoning.

Documents 1 and 2 describe the combination of factors influencing the decisions of African Americans to leave the South. The Supreme Court ruling in Plessy v. Ferguson ushered in a new era of "separate but equal" Jim Crow segregation laws. In Document 1 the National Association for the Advancement of Colored People (NAACP) forcefully spelled out how the South's rigid color line deprived black citizens equal justice, denied them equal treatment on public transportation, and forced their children to attend inferior public schools. In Document 2, the Tuskegee Conference acknowledged the temptation to take jobs in Northern factories. But the Conference reminded its Southern black audience that the wartime industrial boom would be "transitory." In contrast, it predicted the emerging Southern economy would offer more "permanent opportunities."

Documents 1 and 2 are accurately described and used as evidence to support the thesis argument.

The discussion presents a valid Historical Situation analysis for Document 1.

The discussion presents a valid Intended Audience analysis for Document 2.

The pull of good jobs and the push of Southern discrimination persuaded over 1.5 million African Americans to move to urban areas in the North. Document 3 provides statistical data documenting the impact of the Great Migration on the population of six major cities. The end of World War I did not stop the Great Migration. Instead, it accelerated during the 1920s causing a dramatic increase in the number of African Americans living in Northern cities.

Document 3 is accurately described and used as evidence to support the thesis argument.

The discussion presents a valid Purpose analysis for Document 3.

African Americans did find new jobs in the North. But the promise of equality and the hope for an end to racial violence proved to be elusive. In Document 4 a "Northern white efficiency expert" offers his fellow industrial managers advice on how "to preserve the peace" between white and African American workers. His report recommends that prudent managers should "create separate washrooms" and other segregated facilities. He believes this pragmatic policy will help employees avoid unwanted clashes. Although not as systematic as Jim Crow segregation, this "certain amount of segregation" represents an important example of continuity in the social and economic experiences of African Americans living in Northern cities.

Document 4 is accurately described and used as evidence to support the thesis argument.

The discussion presents a valid Intended Audience analysis for Document 4.

The problems experienced by African American migrants were not limited to workplace discrimination. Although African Americans did find new homes in Northern cities, they soon encountered the harsh realities of trying to establish new lives. The surging population of African Americans sparked growing tensions with the white population. Document 5 provides a newspaper description of a race riot that exploded in Chicago's South Side during the summer of 1919. *The Chicago Tribune* account

Document 5 is accurately described and used as evidence to support the thesis argument.

described the beginning of a violent week of racial clashes that left scores dead along with widespread destruction of black homes. Document 5 thus corroborates the warning by the Tuskegee Conference in Document 2.

The discussion presents a valid <u>Historic Situation</u> analysis for Document 5.

Documents 4 and 5 underscore continuities in the social and economic lives of African Americans living in Northern cities. In contrast, Documents 6 and 7 offer a very different cultural perspective. During the 1920s, Harlem became the vibrant center of an outpouring of African American literary, artistic, and musical expression known as the Harlem Renaissance. In Document 6, Marcus Garvey proclaimed the birth of a new black consciousness based upon racial pride. He urged African Americans to join the Universal Negro Improvement Association (UNIA) and participate in a cause devoted to striking down racial barriers. Garvey's galvanizing ideas helped inspire the birth of the "New Negro" movement led by Alain Leroy Locke. In Document 7, Locke proudly described Harlem as "the greatest Negro community the world has known." His vision of a New Negro inspired the principle of "self-determination," reinforced Garvey's message of black pride, and pointed the way to a new black cultural identity.

The Harlem Renaissance is presented as relevant <u>Outside Information</u>.

Documents 6 and 7 are accurately described and used as evidence to support the thesis argument.

The discussion presents a valid <u>Purpose</u> analysis for Document 6.

The discussion presents a valid <u>Purpose</u> analysis for Document 7.

The Great Migration produced far-reaching changes in the African American experience. Although some forms of discrimination continued in the North, African American migrants proudly challenged the racial color line by asserting a more confident cultural identity as "New Negroes."

A concise conclusion restates the nuanced thesis.

COMMENTARY

This model essay would receive all 7 rubric points. Paragraph 1 opens with a combo paragraph that describes the historic context and establishes a nuanced line of reasoning. The essay groups Documents 1 and 2 and Documents 6 and 7 into unified paragraphs. The essay demonstrates a complex understanding by describing the relationship between Documents 2 and 5. It also points out how Documents 4 and 5 and Documents 6 and 7 offer contrasting insights into the processes of continuity and change. The concluding paragraph provides a brief but effective restatement of the thesis.

SCORING SUMMARY

CONTEXTUALIZATION	1 point	Sentences 1 - 4 establish the relevant historic context.
THESIS	1 point	Sentences 5 – 6 provide a sophisticated and nuanced thesis.
DOCUMENT CONTENT	2 points	The content of six documents is used to support the thesis.
EVIDENCE BEYOND THE DOCUMENTS	1 point	The discussion of the Harlem Renaissance in paragraph 6 is relevant to understanding the concepts of black pride and the New Negro.
ANALYSIS (HAPPY)	1 point	Essay identifies the purpose of Docs 3, 6, and 7; the historic situation for Docs 1, and 5; and the intended audience for Docs 2 and 4.
COMPLEXITY	1 point	Essay begins with a sophisticated and nuanced thesis. Documents 2 and 5 talk to each other. The concluding paragraph summarizes the thesis argument.
	7 points	

CHAPTER 8
THE COLD WAR
1943 – 1963

PROMPT

Evaluate the extent of change in the relationship between the United States and the Soviet Union from 1943 to 1963.

DOCUMENT 1

Source: President Franklin D. Roosevelt, Fireside Chat on the Tehran Conference, December 24, 1943

"After the Cairo conference, Mr. Churchill and I went by airplane to Tehran. There we met with Marshall Stalin. We talked with complete frankness on every conceivable subject connected with the winning of the war and the establishment of a durable peace after the war. Within three days of intense and consistently amicable discussions, we agreed on every conceivable subject connected with the launching of a gigantic attack upon Germany.... We did discuss international relationships from the point of view of big, broad objectives, rather than details. But on the basis of what we did discuss, I can say even today that I do not think any insoluble differences will arise among Russia, Great Britain, and the United States."

DOCUMENT 2

Source: Henry Wallace, "The Way to Peace," September 12, 1946

"Getting tough never brought anything real and lasting – whether for schoolyard bullies or businessmen our world powers. The tougher we get, the tougher the Russians will get...The real peace treaty we now need is between the United States and Russia. On our part, we should recognize that we have no more business in the political affairs of Eastern Europe than Russia has in the political affairs of Latin America, Western Europe, and the United States. We may not like what Russia does in Eastern Europe. Her type of land reform, industrial expropriation, and suppression of basic liberties offends the great majority of the people of the United States. But whether we like it or not the Russians will try to socialize their sphere of influence just as we try to democratize our sphere of influence...By mutual agreement, this competition should be put on a friendly basis and the Russians should stop conniving against us in certain areas of the world just as we should stop scheming against them in other parts of the world."

DOCUMENT 3

Source: President Harry S. Truman, address before a joint session of Congress

Articulating what would become known as the Truman Doctrine, March 12, 1947

"Totalitarian regimes imposed upon free peoples by direct or indirect aggression, undermine the foundations of international peace, and hence the security of the United States...At the present moment of world history nearly every nation must choose between alternative ways of life. The choice is often not a free one. One way of life is based upon the will of the majority, and is distinguished by free institutions, representative government, free elections, guarantees of individual liberty, freedom of speech and religion, and freedom from political oppression. The second way of life is based upon the will of a minority imposed upon the majority. It relies upon terror and oppression, a controlled press and radio, fixed elections, and the suppression of personal freedom. I believe it must be the policy of the United States to support free peoples who are resisting attempted subjugation by armed minorities or by outside pressures."

DOCUMENT 4

Source: TIME Magazine, January 6, 1958

"The symbols of 1957 were two pale, clear streaks of light that slashed across the world's night skies and a Vanguard rocket topping into a roiling mass of flame on a Florida beach.

With the *Sputniks* Russia took man into a new era of space, and with its advances in the art of missilery, posed the U.S. with the most dramatic military threat it had ever faced. And with the Vanguard's witlessly ballyhooed crash at Cape Canaveral went the U.S.'s long-held tenet that anything Communism's driven men could do, free men could do better. Whatever the future might bring, in 1957 the U.S. had been challenged and bested in the very area of technological achievement that had made it the world's greatest power."

DOCUMENT 5

Source: Kitchen Debate, Vice-President Richard Nixon and Soviet Premier Nikita Khrushchev, American exhibit in Moscow, July 24, 1959

Nixon: I want to show you this kitchen. It is like those of our houses in California. [Nixon points to the dishwasher]

Khrushchev: We have such things.

Nixon: This house can be bought for $14,000, and most American [veterans from World War II] can buy a home in the bracket of $10,000 to $15,000…

Khrushchev: In Russia, all you have to do to get a house is to be born in the Soviet Union. You are entitled to housing…In America, if you don't have a dollar you have a right to choose between sleeping in a house or on the pavement. Yet you say we are the slave to Communism.

Nixon: This exhibit was not designed to astound but to interest. Diversity, the right to choose, the fact that we have 1,000 builders building 1,000 different houses is the most important thing. We don't have one decision made at the top by one government official. This is the difference.

Khrushchev: We haven't quite reached 42 years, and in another 7 years, we'll be at the level of America, and after that we'[ll go farther. As we pass you by, we'll wave 'hi' to you, and then if you want, we'll stop and say, 'please come along behind us.'"

DOCUMENT 6

Source: Leslie G. Illingworth, The Daily Mail, October 29, 1962

DOCUMENT 7

Source: President John F. Kennedy, Commencement speech at American University, June 10, 1963

Let us re-examine our attitude towards the Cold War, remembering we're not engaged in a debate, seeking to pile up debating points. We are not here distributing blame or pointing the finger of judgment. We must deal with the world as it is, and not as it might have been had the history of the last 18 years been different...Chairman Khrushchev, Prime Minister Macmillan, and I have agreed that high-level discussions will shortly begin in Moscow looking towards early agreement on a comprehensive test ban treaty....To make clear our good faith and solemn convictions on this matter, I now declare that the United States does not propose to conduct nuclear tests in the atmosphere so long as other states do not do so. We will not be the first to resume."

ORGANIZATIONAL CHART

	Sources	Continuity	Change	HAPPY Analysis
Document 1	Presidential Fireside Chat		Wartime allies	Intended audience
Document 2	Speech by cabinet member		Peaceful coexistence	Purpose
Document 3	Presidential address to Congress	Rivalry - containment of Soviet aggression		Purpose
Document 4	Popular news magazine	Rivals in space		Point of view
Document 5	Kitchen debate	Economic rivals		Point of view
Document 6	Political cartoon	Nuclear confrontation		Historic situation
Document 7	Presidential address on Nuclear Test Ban		Peaceful coexistence	

SAMPLE ANNOTATED ESSAY

The Allied victory over Nazi Germany was not enough to end decades of mistrust between the United States and the Soviet Union. A Cold War soon broke out between the two rival superpowers. The global struggle featured both significant changes and continuities. Although examples of peaceful coexistence did take place, in the end Cold War tensions between the United States and the Soviet Union remained a constant part of international relations from 1947 to 1963.

Thesis: The thesis makes a clear defensible claim that establishes a nuanced line of reasoning.

The Cold War was a prolonged period of economic, political, and military rivalry between the United States and the Soviet Union. The Cold War had deep historic roots. In 1917, Bolsheviks led by Vladimir Lenin overthrew the Russian government and transformed the country into a communist dictatorship. The United States did not recognize the newly created Soviet Union until 1933.

Contextualization: Useful background information relates the topic of the prompt to broader events in the earlier relationship between the U.S. and the Soviet Union.

The Second World War forced the United States and the Soviet Union into a temporary alliance to defeat Nazi Germany. The Tehran Conference marked the first meeting of the "Big Three" – FDR, Churchill, and Stalin. The intended audience for FDR's Fireside Chat (Doc 1) was the American public. FDR hoped to reassure nervous Americans that the meeting with Stalin produced "amicable discussions" on the military plans to defeat Hitler. FDR predicted that no "insoluble differences will arise among Russia, Great Britain, and the United States."

Document 1 is accurately described and used as evidence to support the thesis.

The discussion presents a valid Intended Audience analysis for Document 1.

FDR's prediction proved to be wrong. Although the Big Three powers did defeat Nazi Germany, FDR's successor Harry Truman failed to reach a settlement with Stalin on the shape of the postwar order in Eastern Europe and especially Germany. As tensions between the two superpowers mounted, Winston Churchill delivered a speech in Fulton, Missouri in which he grimly warned Americans that "an Iron Curtain has descended across the continent." The once-independent nations of Eastern Europe were fast becoming satellites controlled by the Soviet Union. As the initial postwar spirit of optimism faded, the two former allies became increasingly suspicious rivals.

The discussion of Churchill's Iron Curtain speech is presented as relevant Outside Information.

Henry Wallace, Truman's Secretary of Commerce, disagreed with Churchill's assessment of the situation in Eastern Europe. In his "The Way to Peace" speech (Doc 2), Wallace offered a more conciliatory policy toward the Soviet Union. He argued that the United States had no more business in Eastern Europe than the Soviets had in Latin America. Wallace hoped to persuade Truman that only mutual trust would enable the United States and the Soviet Union to establish peaceful relations.

Document 2 is accurately described and used as evidence to support the thesis argument.

The discussion presents a valid Purpose analysis for Document 2.

Events in Greece and Turkey forced Truman to make a decision. Both nations faced imminent threats from Soviet pressure. Truman responded by asking Congress to pledge $400 million to support the Greek and Turkish governments. However, his address to Congress (Doc 3) went far beyond the short-term purpose of asking for money. Truman's primary purpose was to assert American leadership of the Free World in a global struggle to contain Soviet expansion. Known as

Document 3 is accurately described and used as evidence to support the thesis argument.

the Truman Doctrine, this policy began an aggressive strategy significantly different from the conciliatory approach favored by Henry Wallace in Document 2.

The Cold War involved more than political and military confrontations. Documents 4 and 5 illustrate how the superpower rivalry extended to outer space and even into home kitchens. Russia's successful launch of its *Sputnik* satellite jolted America's self-confidence. TIME Magazine expressed the national mood of humiliation and sense of urgency (Doc 4) when the widely read newsmagazine grimly warned that America had fallen behind in the space race. In Document 5, Vice-President Nixon and Soviet Premier Khrushchev did not debate space satellites. Instead, the two leaders used their so-called "Kitchen Debate" as a platform to express their rival viewpoints about the relative advantages and disadvantages of capitalist and communist economic systems. The abundance or scarcity of consumer products thus became another front in the ongoing Cold War rivalry.

The Cold War confrontation between the United States and the Soviet Union reached a dangerous climax during the Cuban Missile Crisis in October 1962. In a daring but risky gamble, Khrushchev secretly allowed Soviet technicians to build nuclear missile sites in Cuba. When U-2 spy planes discovered the missiles, President Kennedy responded by announcing a naval blockade of Cuba while also threatening to order a massive military invasion of the island. The political cartoon in Document 6 captures the dangerous

The discussion presents a valid <u>Purpose</u> analysis of Document 3.

Documents 4 and 5 are accurately described and used as evidence to support the thesis argument.

The discussion presents a valid <u>Point of View</u> analysis for Document 4.

The discussion presents a valid <u>Point of View</u> analysis for Document 5.

Document 6 is accurately described and used as evidence to support the thesis.

The discussion presents a valid <u>Historic Situation</u> analysis for Document 6.

nuclear test of strength between JFK and Khrushchev. Both leaders are depicted sitting on nuclear bombs. And both appear ready to press buttons that will detonate the bombs and trigger a nuclear holocaust.

The catastrophic danger posed by the Cuban Missile Crisis forced American and Soviet leaders to relax Cold War tensions. Just eight months after the two superpowers approached the brink of a nuclear catastrophe, a somber President Kennedy delivered a speech opening the possibility of initiating a "comprehensive test ban treaty" to begin a new period of peaceful coexistence (Doc 7) Kennedy's intended global audience of concerned nations and peoples welcomed his proposal.

Document 7 is accurately described and used as evidence to support the thesis.

The discussion presents a valid Intended Audience analysis for Document 7.

The test ban treaty did help to reduce Cold War tensions. However, the underlying differences between the United States and the Soviet Union did not go away. As a result, the two superpowers remained rivals until the fall of the Soviet Union in 1991.

A concise conclusion restates the thesis.

COMMENTARY

This model essay would receive all 7 rubric points. Paragraph 1 presents a sophisticated thesis that establishes a nuanced line of reasoning. Paragraph 2 establishes the historic context for understanding relations between the United States and the Soviet Union. The essay presents Documents 1, 2, 3, 6, and 7 in separate paragraphs. However, the essay groups Documents 4 and 5 into one paragraph. The concluding paragraph provides a brief but effective restatement of the thesis.

SCORING SUMMARY

THESIS	1 point	Paragraph 1 provides a sophisticated thesis that establishes a nuanced approach to both continuity and change.
CONTEXTUALIZATION	1 point	Paragraph 2 establishes the historic context.
DOCUMENT CONTENT	2 points	The essay uses all seven documents to support the thesis.
EVIDENCE BEYOND THE DOCUMENTS	1 point	The discussion of Churchill's Iron Curtain speech in paragraph 4 provides relevant background information that contrasts with Wallace's position in paragraph 5 and helps introduce the Truman Doctrine in paragraph 6.
ANALYSIS (HAPPY)	1 point	The essay identifies the purpose of Documents 2 and 3; the point of view of Document 4 and 5; the historic situation for Document 6; and the intended audience for Documents 1 and 7.
COMPLEXITY	1 point	The essay begins with a sophisticated thesis that addresses both continuity and change. It provides in-depth analysis that includes grouping Documents 4 and 5. The concluding paragraph provides a succinct restatement of the thesis.
	7 points	

UNIT III
CAUSATION

CHAPTER 9
INTRODUCING CAUSATION

APUSH teachers frequently ask their students to evaluate the causes and/or effects of a specific historical development or process. For example, what caused the American Revolution? Or what were the effects of the American Revolution? Many students answer the first question by saying, "King George III – he did it!" Or they answer the second question by saying, "America won its independence."

Both of these answers illustrate a simplistic approach to causation. Historians recognize that no single cause or effect explains a historical event or development. The words "cause" or "effect" are convenient figures of speech for a number of factors which help explain why a historical event occurred and what were its enduring consequences.

When studying historical events such as the American Revolution, APUSH students should be prepared to explain the relative importance of different causes and effects. For example, changes in British economic policies and the influence of ideas about natural rights both played a role in causing the American Revolution. The Revolution had very different effects on colonial merchants, women, and enslaved Africans.

RECOGNIZING A CAUSATION DBQ PROMPT

The historical process of causation plays an important role in DBQ questions. During the past few years about one-fourth of all DBQ prompts have asked students to demonstrate their ability to use this historical thinking skill. Here are three examples:

1. Evaluate the relative importance of effects which resulted from the Second Great Awakening during the period between 1800 and 1850.

2. Evaluate the relative importance of different causes of the Civil War in the period from 1830 to 1861.

3. Evaluate the relative importance of different causes for the expanding role of the United States in the world in the period from 1865 to 1910.

Note that DBQ prompts typically use the phrase "evaluate the relative importance of different" to introduce a causation prompt.

CREATING AN ORGANIZATIONAL CHART

The College Board recommends that you devote about 15 minutes to reading and analyzing the seven DBQ documents. Many students find it helpful to create a chart to help them organize their thoughts and keep track of the documents. The sample chart below contains columns for Sources, three Causes/Effects, and HAPPY Analysis.

Writing a DBQ essay requires great concentration. Given the time pressure, it is easy to lose track of the documents and the key points you want to make. An organizational chart can serve as a valuable reference as you write your DBQ essay.

	Sources	Cause/ Effect	Cause/ Effect	Cause/ Effect	HAPPY Analysis
Document 1					
Document 2					
Document 3					
Document 4					
Document 5					
Document 6					
Document 7					

CHAPTER 10
EXPANDING THE SUFFRAGE
1820 – 1848

PROMPT

Evaluate the relative effects of the expansion of the suffrage from 1820 to 1848.

DOCUMENT 1

VOTER PARTICIPATION IN PRESIDENTIAL ELECTIONS

Year	Popular Vote	Percent of Eligible Voter Participation
1820	87,343	10.1
1824	113,142	26.9
1828	642,806	57.3
1832	702,735	57.0
1836	763,291	56.5
1840	1,275,583	80.3
1844	1,360,235	79.2

DOCUMENT 2

Source: James Kent, Chief Justice of the New York State Supreme Court, Excerpt from the Proceedings and Debates of the Convention Assembled for the Purpose of Amending the Constitution of the State of New York, 1821.

The tendency of universal suffrage is to jeopardize the rights of property and the principles of liberty. There is a constant tendency in human society, and the history of every age proves it; there is a tendency in the poor to covet and to share the plunder of the rich; in the debtor, to relax or avoid the obligation of contracts; in the majority, to tyrannize over the minority and trample down their rights; in the indolent and the profligate, to cast the whole burdens of society upon the industrious and virtuous; and there is a tendency in ambitious and wicked me to inflame these combustible materials…

DOCUMENT 3

Source: David Buel, a lawyer and public official, Excerpt from the Proceedings and Debates of the Convention Assembled for the Purpose of Amending the Constitution Assembled for the Purpose of Amending the Constitution of the State of New York, 1821.

When our constitution was framed the domain of the state was in the hands of a few. The proprietors of the great manors were almost the only men of great influence; and the landed property was deemed worthy of almost exclusive consideration. Before the Revolution, freeholders only were allowed to exercise the right of suffrage…It is supposed by the honorable member before me (Chief Justice Kent) that landed property will become insecure under the proposed extension of the right of suffrage, by the influx of a more dangerous population…

I contend that by the true principle of our government, property, as such, is not the basis of representation. Our community is an association of persons – of human beings – not a partnership founded on property….Property is only one of the incidental rights of the person who possesses it; and, as such, it must be made secure, but it does not follow, that it must therefore be represented specifically in any branch of the government.

DOCUMENT 4

Source: Margaret Bayard Smith, eyewitness description of the inauguration of Andrew Jackson, March 4, 1829

The day was warm and delightful, from the South Terrace we had a view of Pennsylvania and Louisiana Avenues, crowded with people hurrying towards the Capitol. It was a most exhilarating scene!...We stood on the South steps of the terrace; when the appointed hour came saw the General and his company advancing up the Avenue, slow, very slow, so impeded was his march by the crowds, thronging around him....The south side of the Capitol hill was literally alive with the multitude, who stood ready to receive the hero, and the multitude who attended him, "There, there, that is he," exclaimed different voices, "Which?" asked others. "There is the old man and his gray hair, there is the old veteran, there is Jackson!"...It was the People's day, and the People's President and the People would rule. God grant that one day or other, the People do not put down all rule and rulers. I fear, enlightened Freemen as they are, they will be found, as they have been found in all ages and countries where they get the Power in their hands, that of all tyrants, they are the most ferocious, cruel, and despotic.

DOCUMENT 5

Source: Davy Crockett, *Colonel Crockett's Exploits and Adventures in Texas*, 1836

When the day of election approaches, visit your constituents far and wide. Treat liberally and drink freely, in order to rise in their estimation, though you fall in your own. True, you may be called a drunken dog by some of the clean-shirt and silk-stocking gentry, but the real roughnecks will style you a jovial fellow. There votes are certain, and frequently count double.

Do all you can to appear to advantage in the eyes of the women. That's easily done. You have but to kiss slobber over their children, wipe their noses, and pat them on the head. This cannot fail to please their mothers...

Promise all that is asked and more if you can think of anything. Offer to build a bridge, or a church, to divide a county, create a batch of new offices, make a turnpike, or anything they like. Promises cost nothing; therefore, deny nobody who has a vote or sufficient influence to obtain one.

DOCUMENT 6

Source: Charles Dickens, English novelist, American Notes for General Circulation, 1842

One great blemish in the popular mind of America, and the prolific parent of an innumerable brood of evils, is Universal Distrust. You [Americans] carry this jealousy and distrust into every transaction of public life. By repelling worthy men from your legislative assemblies, it has bred up a class of candidates for the suffrage, who, in their very act, disgrace your institutions and your people's choice…Any man who attains a high place among you, from the President downwards, may date his downfall from that moment; for any printed lie that any notorious villain pens, although it militate directly against the character and conduct of life, appeals at once to your distrust, and is believed.

DOCUMENT 7

Source: Elizabeth Cady Stanton, Seneca Falls Declaration of Sentiments and Resolutions, 1848.

The history of mankind is a history of repeated injuries and usurpations on the part of man toward woman, having in direct object the establishment of an absolute tyranny over her. To prove this, let facts be submitted to a candid world.

He has never permitted her to exercise her inalienable right to the elective franchise. He has compelled her to submit to laws, in the formation of which she had no voice. He has withheld her rights which are given to the most ignorant and degraded men – both natives and foreign.

Having deprived her of this first right of a citizen, the elective franchise, thereby leaving her without representation in the halls of legislation, he has opposed her on all sides…

Resolved, That it is the duty of the women of this country to secure to themselves their sacred right to the elective franchise.

ORGANIZATIONAL CHART

	Sources	Common Man	Electioneering	Women	HAPPY Analysis
Document 1	Statistical chart	Documents expansion of suffrage			Purpose
Document 2	Opponent of expanded suffrage	Warning of dangers			Point of view
Document 3	Supporter of expanded suffrage	Points out benefits			Point of view
Document 4	Eyewitness description	People's president but			Point of view
Document 5	Crockett's advice		Populist style of electioneering		Intended audience
Document 6	Dickens' criticisms		Inferior candidates		Point of view
Document 7	Public declaration			Demand women's suffrage	Purpose

SAMPLE ANNOTATED ESSAY

The Framers of the Constitution believed that voting rights should be restricted to a natural aristocracy of propertied gentlemen. They therefore limited the franchise to prosperous merchants and wealthy planters who had an economic stake in the government. As a result, property requirements prevented most citizens from voting. However, the early nineteenth century market revolution created a middle class of shopkeepers and craftsmen who demanded a greater voice in running government affairs. The period between 1820 and 1848 witnessed a remarkable expansion of voting rights to include virtually all white men over the age of 21. This expanded electorate had a dramatic effect on the political importance of the common man, the emergence of new styles of electoral campaigning, and the frustrated aspirations of women. Although the rise of the common man and new forms of electioneering were important, in the end the creation of a white man's democracy that denied the franchise to women had the most lasting impact upon American society.

Contextualization: Useful background information in sentences 1 – 4 relates the topic to broader historic trends from 1790 to 1820.

Thesis: The thesis in sentences 5 – 7 makes a clear defensible claim that establishes a nuanced line of reasoning.

During the three decades following George Washington's inauguration, state governments retained property requirements intended to prevent poor people from voting. Documents 1, 3, and 4 highlight steps in the process by which expansion of voting rights spurred the rise of the "common man" in American politics. In Document 3, Daniel Buel delivers a speech to his fellow New York legislators in which he forcefully argues that the right of suffrage should not be solely based upon property. Instead, he offers the alternative point of view that a political community is "an

Documents 1, 3 and 4 are accurately described and used as evidence to support the thesis argument.

The discussion presents a valid Point of View analysis for Document 3.

association of persons" and not exclusively property holders. Buel's argument prevailed in New York and other states. Document 1 provides statistical data documenting the remarkable expansion of democratic participation from just 10.1 percent of eligible voters in 1820 to 80.3 percent in 1840. Document 4 provides Margaret Smith's eyewitness description of the inauguration of Andrew Jackson. For Smith and many Americans, Jackson's rise to the presidency symbolized the rise of the common man in American politics. Although Smith acknowledged that it was "the People's day," she warned that the common man's rise to the top of the American political system could ultimately lead to a form of tyranny.

> The discussion presents a valid <u>Purpose</u> analysis for Document 1.

> The discussion presents a valid <u>Point of View</u> analysis for Document 4.

Jackson's victory in the 1828 presidential election marked the end of the era of Good Feelings and the beginning of a political era dominated by the rise of the common man. Margaret Bayard Smith (Document 4) was not the only worried contemporary observer. In Document 2, James Kent voiced strong opposition to universal suffrage. Kent warned his fellow New York Assembly legislators that debtors and the impoverished majority would "trample down" the rights of creditors and other successful citizens. Although Kent failed to persuade his fellow lawmakers, his worries about the effects of extending the suffrage did not disappear. In 1842, the famed English novelist and social critic Charles Dickens published his observations about the new American electorate. In Document 6, Dickens charged that popular "jealousy and distrust" repelled "worthy men" from running for office, while simultaneously attracting a class of inferior candidates. Easily swayed by any printed lie, naive voters elected unscrupulous candidates who then predictably "disgrace your institutions."

> Documents 2 and 6 are accurately described and used as evidence to support the thesis argument.

> The discussion presents a valid <u>Point of View</u> analysis for Document 2.

> The discussion presents a valid <u>Point of View</u> analysis for Document 6.

Davy Crockett anticipated Dickens' trenchant criticism. The popular Tennessee frontiersman recognized that the expansion of voting rights required a new style of political campaigning. In Document 5, Crockett advises his intended audience of candidates for public office to kiss babies, make extravagant promises, and provide voters with generous quantities of hard cider. Whig Party leaders took Crockett's advice seriously. In the 1840 presidential election the Whigs united behind William Henry Harrison, a wealthy former general who actually lived on a plantation. Whig supporters cleverly recast Harrison as a self-made man who grew up in a log cabin and loved nothing better than drinking hard cider. Their log cabin and hard cider campaign worked as Harrison won the presidential election with the support of a record 80.3 percent of all eligible voters.

The election of 1840 marked the triumph of the dramatic expansion of voting rights to virtually all white men. However, the political community of white men did not include women. Written by Elizabeth Cady Stanton, the Seneca Falls Declaration of Sentiments and Resolutions protests the discrepancy between the language of equality in the Declaration of Independence and the denial of voting rights to American women (Document 7). The refusal to extend voting rights to women deprived America of the political voice and wisdom of half the nation's population.

The rise of the common man and the new style of populist electioneering marked historic effects of the expansion of voting rights between 1824 and 1848. However, the denial of voting rights to women tainted these achievements.

Document 5 is accurately described and used as evidence to support the thesis.

The discussion presents a valid Intended Audience for Document 5.

The 1840 log cabin and hard cider presidential campaign is presented as relevant Outside Information.

Document 7 is accurately described and used as evidence to support the thesis.

The discussion presents a valid Purpose analysis for Document 7.

A concise conclusion restates the thesis.

COMMENTARY

This model essay would receive all 7 rubric points. Paragraph 1 opens with a combo paragraph that describes the historic context and presents a thesis establishing a nuanced line of reasoning. The essay groups Documents 1, 3, and 4, and Documents 2 and 6 into unified paragraphs. The essay demonstrates a complex understanding by contrasting the point of view of documents 2 and 3. It also points out how Document 5 corroborates the point of view in Document 6. The discussion of Document 7 offers a counterpoint to the positive effects of the expansion of the suffrage. The concluding paragraph provides a brief but effective restatement of the thesis.

SCORING SUMMARY

CONTEXTUALIZATION	1 point	Sentences 1 - 4 establish the relevant historic context.
THESIS	1 point	Sentences 5 – 7 provide a sophisticated and nuanced thesis.
DOCUMENT CONTENT	2 points	The content of six documents is used to support the thesis.
EVIDENCE BEYOND THE DOCUMENTS	1 point	The discussion of the election of 1840 in paragraph 4 is relevant to understanding the effect of the new style of electioneering.
ANALYSIS (HAPPY)	1 point	Essay identifies the purpose of Docs 1 and 7; the point of view of Documents 2, 3, 4, and 6; and the intended audience for Document 5.
COMPLEXITY	1 point	Essay begins with a sophisticated and nuanced thesis. Documents 5 and 6 talk to each other. The concluding paragraph summarizes the thesis argument.
	7 points	

CHAPTER 11

THE ENVIRONMENT AND NATURAL RESOURCES 1960 – 1980

PROMPT

Evaluate the relative importance of the causes of the rise of an environmental movement in the period between 1960 and 1980.

DOCUMENT 1

Source: Rachel Carson, *Silent Spring*, 1962

There was once a town in the heart of America where all life seemed to live in harmony with its surroundings...Then a strange blight crept over the area and new kinds of sickness appeared...There was a strange silence...The birds... where had they gone? Hens brooded, but no chicks hatched. The farmers were unable to raise any pigs. Apple trees were coming into bloom, but no bees droned among the blossoms...

The history of life on earth has been a history of interaction between living things and their surroundings. To a large extent, the physical form and the habits of the earth's vegetation and its animal life have been molded by the environment...The most alarming of all man's assaults upon the environment is the contamination of air, earth, rivers, and sea with dangerous and even lethal [chemical] materials...

I contend, furthermore, that we have allowed these chemicals to be used with little or no advance investigation of their effect on soil, water, wildlife, and man himself. Future generations are unlikely to condone our lack of prudent concern for the integrity of the natural world that supports all life.

DOCUMENT 2

Source: "Earthrise," photograph taken by astronaut William Anders, December 24, 1968, Apollo 8, NASA.

DOCUMENT 3

Source: Kathy Morales, high school student, February 3, 1969, *Black Tide, The Santa Barbara, Oil Spill and Its Consequences*, 1972

I saw a dying loon covered from head to foot with black, sticky crude oil. You want to talk about the Establishment? This is my life – out here. I come out here all the time to watch the sea and the birds and animals. I can't think of coming down here for a stroll again. I can't think of someday bringing my children here to watch and play. I don't know now, if it will ever be the same again and no one remove the tears on my face.

DOCUMENT 4

Source: The Environmental Teach-In, Inc., Ad in the *Sunday New York Times*, January 18, 1970

A disease has infected our country. It has brought smog to Yosemite, dumped garbage in the Hudson, sprayed DDT in our food, and left our cities in decay. Its carrier is man...

On April 22 we stand to reclaim the environment we have wrecked. April 22 is the Environmental Teach-In, a day of environmental action. Hundreds of communities and campuses across the country are already committed...Earth Day is a commitment to make life better, not just bigger and faster. To provide real rather than rhetorical solutions...It is a day to challenge the corporate and government leaders who promise change, but who short change the necessary programs. It is a day for looking beyond tomorrow. April 22 seeks a future worth living.

DOCUMENT 5

Source: President Richard Nixon, State of the Union message to Congress, January 22, 1970.

The great question of the 1970s is, shall we surrender and begin to make reparations for the damage we have done to our air to our land, and to our water? Restoring nature to its natural state is a cause beyond party and beyond factions. It has become a common cause of all the people in this country... Clean air, clean water, open spaces – these shall once again be the birthright of every American. If we act now, they will.

We still think of air as free. But clean air is not free, and neither is clean water. The price tag on pollution control is high. Through our years of past carelessness we incurred a debt to nature, and now that debt is being called. The program I shall purpose to Congress will be the most comprehensive and costly program in this field in America's history.

DOCUMENT 6

Source: President Jimmy Carter, Keeping Faith, 1980

The Superfund legislation may prove to be as far-reaching and important as any accomplishment of my administration. The reduction of the threat to America's health and safety from thousands of toxic-waste sites will continue to be an urgent issue.

DOCUMENT 7

Source: Randy Newman, lyrics from "Burn On, Big River," 1972. Newman's song is a lyrical response to the Cuyahoga River fire on June 22, 1969.

There's a red moon rising on the Cuyahoga River
Rolling into Cleveland to the lake…

There's an oil barge winding down the Cuyahoga River
Rolling into Cleveland to the lake…

Cleveland, city of light, city of magic
Cleveland, city of light you're calling me…

Cleveland even now I can remember
Cause the Cuyahoga River goes smoking through my dreams…

Burn on, big river, burn on
Burn on big river, burn on…

Now the Lord can make you tumble
The Lord can make you turn
The Lord can make you overflow
But the Lord can't make you burn

ORGANIZATIONAL CHART

	Sources	Public Awareness	Ecological Disasters	Presidential Leadership	HAPPY Analysis
Document 1	*Silent Spring*	Bestselling book			Purpose
Document 2	NASA photograph	Image of Earth from the lunar surface			Intended audience
Document 3	Eyewitness reaction		Santa Barbara oil spill		Historic situation
Document 4	Newspaper ad	Promote Earth Day			Intended Audience
Document 5	State of the Union address			Nixon calls for action	Purpose
Document 6	Presidential memoir			Superfund	Purpose
Document 7	Popular song		Cuyahoga River fire		Point of view

SAMPLE ANNOTATED ESSAY

During the Gilded Age, Americans largely ignored their shortsighted and unchecked exploitation of the nation's natural resources. Led by Progressive reformers, the Roosevelt administration adopted preservationist and conservationist measures to protect America's threatened environment. Although these actions reversed some of the environmental damage, their impact faded as public attention shifted to surviving the Great Depression and winning World War II. The postwar period produced unprecedented prosperity and a renewed assault on the environment. A combination of a new ecological awareness, a series of highly publicized environmental disasters, and timely presidential leadership gave rise to a renewed and successful environmental movement. Although growing public awareness and a series of environmental catastrophes were important, in the end presidential leadership proved to be decisive.

Documents 1, 2, and 4 identify key steps in the public's growing awareness of the potentially disastrous consequences of ignoring the environment. Document 1 presents an excerpt from Rachel Carson's landmark book *Silent Spring*. Carson's book awakened the American people to the deadly consequences of the unrestricted use of synthetic chemicals like DDT. *Silent Spring* was more than a study of the effects of pesticides; it was also an indictment of America's blind faith in scientific progress. *Silent Spring* sold 2 million copies and helped galvanize a growing environmental movement based upon the ecological principle that all living plants and animals are part of an interdependent web of life. Known as *Earthrise*, the famous image in

Contextualization: Useful background information in sentences 1 – 4 relates the topic of the prompt to broader historic developments.

Thesis: The thesis in sentences 5 and 6 makes a clear defensible claim that establishes a nuanced line of reasoning.

Documents 1, 2, and 4 are accurately described and used as evidence to support the thesis argument.

The discussion presents a valid Purpose analysis for Document 1.

Document 2 underscored Carson's fundamental message about the beauty and fragility of life on Earth. Taken from lunar orbit by Apollo 8 astronaut William Anders, NASA released *Earthrise* to a global audience enabling the image to become one of the most viewed pictures in history. The growing environmental awareness reached a climax on Earth Day. First proposed by Senator Gaylord Nelson as an environmental teach-in, the idea soon took on a life of its own. The ad excerpted in Document 4 appealed to an intended audience of concerned citizens to contribute time and donate money to make Earth Day a success.

Documents 3 and 7 present compelling responses to shocking ecological disasters that jarred the American public. In late January 1969 an oil rig explosion in the Santa Barbara Channel created an oil slick that turned miles of pristine Southern California beaches into an environmental nightmare. In Document 3, a distraught high school student responds to the painful sight of a black tide fouling her favorite beach and killing defenseless birds. Kathy Morales' anguished cry became part of a national protest demanding stricter environmental regulations. Just six months later another shocking environmental disaster further galvanized public opinion. The Cuyahoga River flows through Cleveland and into Lake Erie. For years, steel mills, oil refineries, chemical companies, and local citizens poured raw sewage, acids, chemicals, and floating debris into the lifeless river.On June 22, 1969 sparks from a passing train landed on the river and ignited a fire. In Document 7, songwriter Randy Newman responds to the absurdity of a river on fire. Newman concludes his song by directly pointing the blame on human negligence.

The discussion presents a valid Intended Audience analysis for Document 2.

The discussion presents a valid Intended Audience analysis for Document 4.

Documents 3 and 7 are accurately described and used as evidence to support the thesis argument.

The discussion presents a valid Historic Situation analysis for Document 3.

The discussion presents a valid Point of View analysis for Document 7.

The Santa Barbara oil spill and the Cuyahoga River fire mobilized public support for new environmental policies. Document 5 demonstrates President Nixon's pivotal role in the rise of the environmental movement. In his first State of the Union address (Doc 5), Nixon pledged vigorous actions to "restoring nature to its natural state." After using the nationally televised speech to build public and congressional support, Nixon successfully supported a package of landmark environmental legislation. For example, he created the Environmental Protection Agency (EPA) to enforce environmental laws, the Clean Air Act to set national air-quality standards, and the Water Pollution Control Act to clean up the nation's polluted rivers. President Carter also demonstrated the crucial importance of presidential leadership in responding to an environmental disaster.

Between 1942 and 1952, the Hooker Chemical Company dumped 20,000 tons of highly toxic chemical waste into an abandoned ditch in the Love Canal section of Niagara Falls, New York. The company lined the site with clay, covered it with dirt, and then sold the land to the Niagara Falls Board of Education for $1.00. During the next two decades, Love Canal became a comfortable working-class neighborhood that included an elementary school built directly over the toxic waste site. During the 1970s, local residents began to report foul odors, dying trees, and disturbingly high rates of miscarriages and birth defects. President Carter responded to the Love Canal crisis by asking Congress for legislation that would create a $1.6 billion Superfund to clean up the Love Canal and other toxic-waste sites across

---

Document 5 is accurately described and used as evidence to support the thesis argument.

The discussion presents a valid Purpose analysis for Document 5.

The background story of the Love Canal toxic waste site is presented as relevant Outside Information.

Document 6 is accurately described and used as evidence to support the thesis argument.

The discussion presents a valid Purpose analysis for Document 6.

America. Document 6 is an excerpt from President Carter's memoirs. Written shortly after he left office, the passage underscores the importance President Carter attached to his role in creating the Superfund.

A combination of growing economic awareness, highly publicized environmental disasters, and decisive presidential leadership gave rise to a renewed environmental movement during the period from 1960 to 1980. Presidents Nixon and Carter provided leadership that transformed public outrage into concrete legislative actions.

A concise conclusion restates the nuanced thesis.

COMMENTARY

This model essay would receive all 7 rubric points. It opens with a combo paragraph that contains historic contextualization and a nuanced thesis. The thesis statement identifies three major causes of the rise of an environmental movement between 1960 and 1980. The essay uses a grouping strategy to discuss each of these causal factors. This enables the essay to make frequent comparisons between the documents. The concluding paragraph provides a brief but effective restatement of the thesis.

SCORING SUMMARY

THESIS	1 point	Paragraph 1 provides a sophisticated thesis that establishes a nuanced approach to historic causation.
CONTEXTUALIZATION	1 point	Paragraph 1 establishes the historic context.
DOCUMENT CONTENT	2 points	The essay uses six documents to support the thesis.
EVIDENCE BEYOND THE DOCUMENTS	1 point	The discussion in paragraph 5 of the Love Canal toxic site provides relevant outside information for Document 6.
ANALYSIS (HAPPY)	1 point	The essay identifies the purpose of Documents 1, 5 and 6; the point of view of Document 7; the intended audience for Documents 2 and 4; and the historic situation for Document 3.
COMPLEXITY	1 point	The essay begins with a sophisticated thesis that creates a nuanced line of reasoning by identifying the relative impact of three causal factors. It provides analysis by devoting a separate paragraph to each causal factor. The conclusion provides a succinct restatement of the thesis.
	7 points	

CHAPTER 12
THE WOMEN'S RIGHTS MOVEMENT 1940 – 1975

PROMPT

Explain the causes of the rise of a women's rights movement in the years between 1940 and 1975.

DOCUMENT 1

Source: Office of War Information, a United States government agency, 1943, Courtesy of the Library of Congress.

DOCUMENT 2

Source: Governor Adlai Stevenson, "A Purpose for Modern Woman," Commencement Address, Smith College, 1955

And here's where you come in: to restore valid, meaningful purpose to life in your home....You may be hitched to one of those creatures we call 'Western man' and I think part of your job is to keep him Western, to keep him truly purposeful, to keep him whole...

This assignment for you, as wives and mothers, has great advantages. In the first place, it is homework, you can do it in the living room with a baby in your lap or in the kitchen with a can opener in your hand. If you're really clever, maybe you can even practice your saving arts on that unsuspecting man while he's watching television!...Women, especially educated women, have a unique opportunity to influence us, man and boy, and to play a direct part in the unfolding drama of our free society....What you have learned and can learn will, fit you for the primary task of making homes and whole human beings in whom the rational values of freedom, tolerance, charity, and free inquiry can take root."

DOCUMENT 3

Source: *The Feminine Mystique*, Betty Friedan, 1963

The problem lay buried, unspoken, for many years in the minds of American women. It was a strange stirring, a sense of dissatisfaction, a yearning that women suffered in the middle of the twentieth century in the United States. Each suburban wife struggled with it alone. As she made the beds, shopped for groceries, matched slipcover material, ate peanut butter sandwiches with her children, chauffeured Cub Scouts and Brownies, lay beside her husband at night – she was afraid to ask even of herself the silent question – "Is this all."

DOCUMENT 4

Source: "Position Paper: November 1964" by Casey Hayden and Mary King

The average SNCC [Student Nonviolent Coordinating Committee] worker finds it difficult to discuss the woman problem because of the assumption of male superiority. Assumptions of male superiority are as widespread and deep rooted and every much as crippling to the woman as the assumptions of white supremacy are to the Negro. Consider why it is in SNCC that women who are competent, qualified, and experienced, are automatically assigned to the "female" kinds of jobs such as typing, desk work, telephone work, filing, library work, cooking, and the assistant kind of administrative work but rarely the "executive" kind…

This paper is presented because it needs to be made known that many women in the movement are not "happy and contented" with their status…Maybe sometime in the future the whole of the women in this movement will become so alert as to force the rest of the movement to stop the discrimination and start the slow process of changing values and ideas so that all of us gradually come to understand that this is no more a man's world than it is a white world.

DOCUMENT 5

Source: "Women's Bill of Rights in 1968," adopted by National Organization of Women (NOW) at its 1967 convention.

We Demand

That equal employment opportunity be guaranteed in all women, as well as men by insisting that the Equal Employment Opportunity Commission enforce the prohibition against sex discrimination in employment under Title VII of the Civil Rights Act of 1964 with the same vigor as it enforces the prohibitions against racial discrimination.

That women be protected by law to insure their rights to return to their jobs within a reasonable time after childbirth without loss of seniority or other accrued benefits and be paid maternity leave as a form of social security and/or employee benefit.

That the right of women to be educated in their full potential equally with men be secured by Federal and State legislation, eliminating all discrimination and segregation by sex, written and unwritten, at all levels of education including college, graduate and professional schools, loans and fellowships, and Federal and State training programs, such as job Corps.

DOCUMENT 6

Source: Robin Morgan and the New York Radical Women, press release, "No More Miss America!," August 22, 1968

FOR IMMEDIATE RELEASE

On September 7th in Atlantic City, the Annual Miss America Pageant will again crown "our ideal." But this year, reality will liberate the contest auction-block... Women of every political persuasion – all are invited to join us in a day-long boardwalk-theater event, starting at 1:00 p.m. on the Boardwalk in front of Atlantic City's Convention Hall. We will protest the image of Miss America, an image that oppresses women in every area in which it purports to represent us. There will be: Picket Lines; Guerrilla Theater; Leafleting; Lobbying Visits to the contestants urging our sisters to reject the Pageant Farce and join us; a huge Freedom Trash Can (into which we will throw bras, girdles, curlers, false eyelashes, wigs, and representative issues of *Cosmopolitan, Ladies Home Journal, Family Circle*, etc.-bring any such woman-garbage you have around the house); we will also announce a Boycott of all those commercial products related to the Pageant; and the day will end with a Women's Liberation rally at midnight when Miss America is crowned on live television. Lots of other surprises are being planned...It should be a groovy day on the Boardwalk in the sun with our sisters.

DOCUMENT 7

Source: United States Congress, Title IX, Education Amendment, 1972

No person in the United States shall, on the basis of sex, be excluded from participation in, be denied the befts of, or be subjected to discrimination under any education program or activity receiving Federal financial assistance.

ORGANIZATIONAL CHART

	Sources	Traditional gender roles	Feminist activists	Federal policies	HAPPY Analysis
Document 1	Goverment poster			Encourage women to perform male jobs	Purpose
Document 2	Commencement address	Supports traditional gender roles			Point of view
Document 3	Popular book	Critique of traditional gender roles			Point of view
Document 4	Position paper		Radical critique		Point of view
Document 5	List of demands		Liberal reforms		Purpose
Document 6	Press release		Radical protest		Purpose
Document 7	Federal legislation			Eliminate gender discrimination in education	Purpose

SAMPLE ANNOTATED ESSAY

A combination of discontent with traditional gender roles, the determined initiatives of feminist activists, and a major legislative initiative by the federal government caused the rise of a second wave of American feminism in the years between 1940 and 1975. Although the reaction against traditional gender roles and the passage of federal legislation were important, in the end the protests of feminists who demanded more equitable treatment of women played the most pivotal role in fueling a vigorous women's rights movement.

Thesis: The thesis makes a clear defensible claim that establishes a nuanced line of reasoning.

American women have confronted inequality since Abigail Adams' famous but futile letter admonishing her husband the future president John Adams to "remember the ladies." The first feminist wave began with the Seneca Falls Convention in 1848 and ended 72 years later with the passage of the Nineteenth Amendment giving women the right to vote. Although much work remained, the women's movement lacked a unifying goal. The self-indulgent materialism of the Roaring Twenties contributed to the disappearance of the women's movement. During the 1930s, the Great Depression forced American women to find jobs and help their families survive desperate economic hardship.

Contextualization: Useful background information relates the topic of the prompt to broader historic developments.

In the years following World War II the nation's fast-growing suburbs became havens for a revived cult of domesticity in which men commuted to work while their wives stayed home and raised their children. Documents 2 and 3 provide contrasting views of this suburban lifestyle. In Document 2, Governor Adlai Stevenson offers the graduating

Documents 2 and 3 are accurately described and used as evidence to support the thesis argument.

class of female Smith College students a traditional view of their social role. According to Stevenson's point of view they should devote all their energy to supporting their husbands and raising their children. It apparently did not occur to Stevenson that the female graduates of Smith College might want to use their advanced education to pursue their own careers. In Document 3, Betty Friedan expresses the dissatisfaction with the suburban goal of being perfect wives and mothers. Published in 1963, *The Feminist Mystique* expressed the unspoken but very real sense of unfulfilled domesticity felt by suburban housewives who spent their days buying groceries, cooking meals, chauffeuring their children and silently asking, "Is this all?" Millions of American women read Friedan's book and agreed with her point of view by answering the unspoken question with a resounding no! Historians credit *The Feminist Mystique* with helping to launch a historic second wave of feminist activism.

The discussion presents a valid Point of View analysis for Document 2.

The discussion presents a valid Point of View analysis for Document 3.

Documents 4, 5, and 6 express aspects of the outrage expressed by a new generation of female activists. In Document 5, the National Organization for Women listed demands designed to improve the lives of American women. As the first women's rights organization formed after suffrage, NOW's demands reflected the goals of liberal feminists who wanted to work within the system to gain legal equality. In contrast, Documents 5 and 6 provide examples of the tactics of radical feminists who called for the elimination of male supremacy. In Document 4, Casey Hayden and Mary King point out that women who hoped to make a difference by joining SNCC and other civil rights organizations faced a deep-rooted male-dominated culture. Written from the point of view of radical feminists, their position paper pointed

Documents 4, 5, and 6 are accurately described and used as evidence to support the thesis argument.

The discussion presents a valid Purpose analysis for Document 5.

The discussion presents a valid Point of View analysis for Document 4.

out the similarities between assumptions of white supremacy and assumptions of male supremacy. Document 6 illustrates the growing sense of unity among radical women activists. Robin Morgan and the New York Radical Women issued a press release inviting women to join the protest of the 1968 Miss America beauty pageant. Their demonstration focused particular attention on how the pageant objectified women as sex objects. The protest's attack on conventional femininity encouraged other concerned women to speak-out and help sway public opinion.

The discussion presents a valid Purpose analysis for Document 6.

The growing feminist movement had a dramatic impact upon federal legislation. Documents 5 and 7 illustrate the link between the goals of the feminist movement and government policy. In Document 5, NOW demanded legislation to eliminate discrimination against women "at all levels of education." Title IX (Doc 7) fulfilled this goal. The legislation led to a Revolution in education by requiring that women's sports be funded at equivalent levels to men's sports. It also placed more pressure on institutions of higher learning to adopt affirmative action policies that led to a dramatic increase in the percentage of women enrolled in medical and law schools. And finally, Title IX encouraged the proliferation of women's studies courses and degree programs.

Document 7 is accurately described and used as evidence to support the thesis argument.

The discussion presents a valid Purpose analysis for Document 7.

The various impacts of Title IX are presented as relevant Outside Information.

Encounters with traditional forms of male dominance produced a growing sense of female frustration and solidarity. Second wave feminist activists achieved notable legislative success while also transforming traditional attitudes toward the role of women in American society.

A concise conclusion restates the nuanced thesis.

COMMENTARY

This model essay would receive all 7 rubric points. It opens with separate paragraphs for a nuanced thesis and for historic contextualization. The thesis statement identifies three major causes of the rise of a feminist movement between 1940 and 1975. The essay uses a grouping strategy to discuss each of these causal factors. This enables the essay to make frequent comparisons between the documents. The concluding paragraph provides a brief but effective restatement of the thesis.

CONTEXTUALIZATION	1 point	Paragraph 1 provides a sophisticated thesis that establishes a nuanced approach to both continuity and change.
THESIS	1 point	Paragraph 2 establishes the historic context.
DOCUMENT CONTENT	2 points	The essay uses six documents to support the thesis.
EVIDENCE BEYOND THE DOCUMENTS	1 point	The discussion in paragraph 5 of the Impact of Title IX provides relevant outside information.
ANALYSIS (HAPPY)	1 point	The essay identifies the purpose of Documents 5, 6, and 7; and the point of view of Documents 2, 3, and 4.
COMPLEXITY	1 point	The essay begins with a sophisticated thesis that creates a nuanced line of reasoning by identifying the relative impact of three causal factors. It provides analysis by devoting a separate paragraph to each causal factor. The conclusion provides a succinct restatement of the thesis.
	7 points	

UNIT IV
THE PLAN B OPTION

CHAPTER 13
THE PLAN B OPTION
RECONSTRUCTION

The DBQ essay is an important part of your APUSH exam. The DBQ rubric (see Chapter 1) contains 7 points. Each of these rubric points is worth 5 exam points. The DBQ is thus worth 35 points or 25 percent of your exam's total of 140 points.

APUSH DBQs are written to challenge even the best students. As a result, the average DBQ scores are low. Between 2017 and 2019 average DBQ scores ranged from a low of 2.22 to a high of 2.54. Remember, 7 is a perfect score.

The low average scores reflect the difficulty of the DBQ assignment. Many students find they do not have enough time. Others complain that prompts test difficult topics and the documents are often obscure and very hard to understand.

THE PLAN B OPTION

Your Plan A should always be to begin by carefully reading the prompt and the seven documents. Hopefully you will be able to write a sophisticated thesis supported by six or even all seven documents. But what if you are unprepared for the prompt and don't understand all the documents? Is there a Plan B option that can help you write a successful essay?

Fortunately, the answer is YES! Plan B is designed to help you earn 4 rubric points. It is important to note that these scores will keep you on track to earn an overall score of a 3 or 4.

PLAN B ANALYSIS

As always, begin by carefully reading the prompt and the documents. But instead of trying to analyze six or seven documents, focus your attention on three documents you can accurately summarize. This will earn your first rubric point.

Now carefully examine the three documents to determine each document's historic setting, intended audience, point of view OR purpose. Your HAPPY analysis will earn a second rubric point.

Now take another look at your three documents. Do any of these documents trigger a recollection of relevant outside information? If so, add a couple sentences identifying and explaining the relevance of this outside information. This will earn you a third rubric point.

Finally, earn a fourth rubric point by beginning your essay with a straightforward thesis that provides the College Board readers with a clear answer to the prompt.

That's it! Four Plan B paragraphs will earn 4 rubric points which equal 20 exam points.

A 4 on your DBQ will make it difficult but not impossible for you to earn an overall score of a 5. But don't panic! It is important to remember that you only need about 72 points to earn a 3 and about 90 points to earn a 4.

THE MIGHTY 3

APUSH students know that 5s and 4s are desirable scores that will impress college admissions officers and earn valuable college credits. But what about a 3? Is it a valuable score? The answer to this question is a resounding YES!

Here is a surprising fact: More than 60 percent of APUSH students now live in states where policymakers have legislated that their public colleges and universities must award college credit to students who score a 3 on any AP exam. For example, Georgia, Colorado, Florida, Minnesota, New York, Ohio, South Carolina, and Virginia all require their state colleges and universities to award college credit for a 3.

But what if you don't live in a state with this requirement? Don't worry! Nationwide, 83 percent of the credit policies at 4-year public institutions award credit for a 3. The 3 is thus a mighty and valuable score that will save you and your family thousands of tuition dollars.

PRACTICE, PRACTICE, PRACTICE

Practice is essential. Your DBQ will not magically write itself. The DBQ from Chapter 6 is reprinted below. Although the seven documents vary in difficulty, you should be able to summarize three of the documents, provide a HAPPY analysis, add relevant outside information, and write a short thesis statement.

The DBQ is followed by a sample Plan B essay. Carefully study the annotated sample essay. Now it's your turn to write a Plan B DBQ essay. Practice is extremely important. It will build your competence and competence will build your confidence. YOU CAN DO IT!

PROMPT

Evaluate the extent of change and continuity in the lives of African Americans in the South during the period 1865 to 1900.

DOCUMENT 1

Source: Carl Schurz, *Report on the Condition of the South*, 1865

There is, at present, no danger of another insurrection against the authority of the United States on a large scale, and the people are willing to reconstruct their State governments, and to send their senators and representatives to Congress. But as to the moral value of these results, we must not indulge in any delusions …. There is, as yet, among the Southern people an utter absence of national feeling…

Aside from the assumption that the Negro will not work without physical compulsion, there appears to be another popular notion… that the Negro exists for the special object of raising cotton, rice, and sugar for the whites, and that it is illegitimate for him to indulge, like other people, in the pursuit of his own happiness in his own way.

DOCUMENT 2

Source: Laws of St. Landry Parish, Louisiana, 1865

No Negro shall be allowed to pass within the limits of said parish without special permit in writing from his employer.

Every Negro is required to be in the regular service of some white person, or former owner, who shall be held responsible for the conduct of said Negro.

No public meeting or congregations of Negroes shall be allowed within said parish after sunset…

No Negro shall be permitted to preach, exhort, or otherwise declaim to congregations of colored people, without special permission in writing from the president of the police jury…

No Negro who is not in the military service shall be allowed to carry firearms, or any kind of weapons, within the parish, without the special written permission of his employer…

It shall be the duty of every citizen to act as a police officer for the detection of offenses and the apprehension of offenders, who shall be immediately handed over to the proper captain or chief of patrol.

DOCUMENT 3

Source: Interview with Henry Blake, African American farmer in Little Rock Arkansas, as part of the Federal Writers' Project, a government program during the Great Depression.

After freedom, we worked on shares a while…When we worked on shares, we couldn't make nothing, just overalls and something to eat. Half went to the other man and you would destroy your half if you weren't careful. A man that didn't know how to count would always lose. He might lose anyhow. They didn't give no itemized statement. No, you just had to take their word. They never gave you no details. They just say you owe so much. No matter how good account you kept, you had to go by their account…They'd keep you in debt… Anything that kept you a slave because he was always right and you were always wrong if there was a difference.

DOCUMENT 4

Source: Fifteenth Amendment to the United States Constitution, 1870

Section 1. The right of citizens of the United States to vote shall not be denied or abridged by the United States or by any state on account of race, color, or previous condition of servitude.

Section 2. The Congress shall have power to enforce this article by appropriate legislation.

DOCUMENT 5

Thomas Nast in *Harper's Weekly*, October 24, 1874, Library of Congress

DOCUMENT 6

Source: Booker T. Washington, "Atlanta Compromise Address",
September 11, 1895

We have proved our loyalty to you in the past, in nursing your children, watching by the sickbed of your mothers and fathers, and often following them with tear-dimmed eyes to their graves, so in the future, in our humble way, we shall stand by you with devotion that no foreigner can approach, ready to lay down our lives, if need be, in defense of yours, interlacing our industrial, commercial, civil, and religious life with yours in a way that shall make the interests of both races one. In all things that are purely social we can be as separate as the fingers, yet one as the hand in all things essential to mutual progress…. The wisest among my race understand that the agitation of questions of social equality is the extremist folly, and that progress in the enjoyment of all the privileges that will come to us must be the result of severe and constant struggle rather than of artificial forcing…The opportunity to earn a dollar in a factory just now is worth infinitely more than the opportunity to spend a dollar in an opera house.

DOCUMENT 7

Source: William A. Sinclair, historian and former slave, *The Aftermath of Slavery*, 1905

Schools were planted: the lower grades; the preparatory schools; the normal schools; the colleges; the professional schools….For a time this work of education was supported by the National Government, supplemented by Northern benevolence and by a nominal fee which was charged the colored parent for each child…As a result of this impetus the colored man can make this showing in a single generation:

Educationally his illiteracy has been cut down forty-seven percent, although there are nearly three times as many colored people today as were emancipated. He fills the common schools with 1,200,000 of his children; 30,000 are in schools for higher learning, and trade schools; over 200 are pursuing studies in Northern universities, or taking special courses in European institutions…It may be noted that 278 colored women are among the graduates of colleges…

ORGANIZATIONAL CHART

	Sources	Continuity	Change	HAPPY Analysis
Document 1	First-person report	Defeated but defiant		Intended audience
Document 2	Legal code	Slavery by another name		Purpose
Document 3	Sharecropper	Cycle of poverty and debt		Point of view
Document 4	Constitutional amendment		Enfranchise black voters	Purpose
Document 5	Political cartoon	Dramatize Klan violence		Point of view
Document 6	Public address	Advocate black self-help and accomodation		Purpose/ Intended audience
Document 7	Historical report		Public education for African Americans	Purpose

ANNOTATED PLAN B ESSAY

The end of the Civil War presented the newly freed slaves with new opportunities and persistent problems. As a result, African Americans experienced a combination of both change and continuity during the period from 1865 to 1900. Although African Americans experienced changes, in the end racial segregation and discrimination continued to dominate their lives.

Thesis: The thesis makes a clear and defensible claim.

Document 2 provides examples of a newly enacted Black Code in St. Landry Parish, Louisiana. The white lawmakers designed the code to preserve a social, economic, and legal system that resembled slavery in everything but name. For example, the code barred blacks from speaking in public, owning firearms, and moving freely within the parish.

Document 2 is accurately described.

The discussion presents a valid Purpose analysis for Document 2.

Document 3 describes the difficulties faced by a former sharecropper. In this system, black farmers exchanged their labor for the use of a planter's land, tools, and seed. As noted by Henry Blake, many of the planters deliberately cheated their sharecroppers. Blake's point of view is clear – sharecropping trapped African American farmers in a seemingly endless cycle of poverty and debt that resembled slavery.

Document 3 is accurately described.

The discussion presents a valid Point of View analysis for Document 3.

Congress passed the Fifteenth Amendment (Doc 5) to give African American men the right to vote. At first, this proved to be a positive gain as African American voters elected a number of Black public officials. But Jim Crow laws soon reversed these gains. Southern governments used literacy tests and poll taxes to evade the amendment and deprive black citizens of their right to vote.

Document 4 is accurately described.

The discussion presents a valid Purpose analysis for Document 4.

The discussion of Jim Crow voting restrictions presented as relevant Outside Information.

COMMENTARY

This model Plan B essay would receive 4 rubric points. The essay opens with a clear thesis that establishes a defensible line of reasoning. Paragraphs 2, 3, and 4 accurately describe Documents 2, 3, and 4. Sourcing information is provided for each of these three documents. And finally, the essay provides relevant outside information for Document 4.

SCORING SUMMARY

THESIS	1 point	Paragraph 1 provides a clear and defensible thesis statement.
CONTEXTUALIZATION	0 points	The essay does not provide a broader historic context.
DOCUMENT CONTENT	1 point	The essay accurately describes the content of three documents.
EVIDENCE BEYOND THE DOCUMENTS	1 point	The discussion of Jim Crow voting restrictions provides relevant outside information.
ANALYSIS (HAPPY)	1 point	The essay identifies the purpose of Documents 2 and 4 and the point of view of Document 3.
COMPLEXITY	0 points	The essay does not meet the criteria required to earn the complexity point.
	4 points	

CHAPTER 14
PLAN B PRACTICE
WESTERN EXPANSION

Chapter 13 introduced and explained the Plan B strategy for earning 4 rubric points on your DBQ. This chapter is designed to provide you with an additional opportunity to practice your ability to write a Plan B DBQ essay.

PROMPT

Evaluate the relative importance of the effects of Western Expansion on the development of the United States from 1830 to 1870.

DOCUMENT 1

Source: John L. O'Sullivan, newspaper editor, *The United States Magazine and Democratic Review*, November 1830

Our national birth was the beginning of a new history, the formation and progress of an untried political system, which separates us from the past and connects us to the future only; and so far as regards the entire rights of man, in moral, political, and national life, we may confidently assume that our country is destined to be the great nation of futurity…We are entering on its untrodden space, with the truths of God in our minds, beneficent objects in our hearts, and a clear conscience unsullied by the past. We are the nation of human progress, and who will, what can, see limits to our onward march?

The far-reaching, the boundless future will be the era of American greatness. In its magnificent domain of space and time, the nation of many nations, is destined to manifest to mankind, the excellence of divine principles…

DOCUMENT 2

Source: Elias Boudinot, influential member of the Cherokee Tribe, *Cherokee Phoenix*, November 1831

But alas! No sooner was it made manifest that the Cherokee were becoming strongly attached to the ways and usages of civilized life, than was aroused the opposition of those from whom better things ought to have been expected. No sooner was it known that they had learned the proper use of the earth, and they were less likely to dispose of their lands for a mess of potage, then they came into conflict with the cupidity and self-interest of those who might have been their benefactors.

Then commenced a series of obstacles hard to overcome, and difficulties intended as a stumbling block, and not thought of before. The "Great Father" [Andrew Jackson] of the "red man" has lent his influence to encourage these difficulties. The guardian has deprived his wards of their rights. The sacred obligations of treaties and laws have been disregarded, the promises of Washington and Jefferson have not been fulfilled. The policy of the United States on Indian affairs has taken a different direction, for no other reason than the Cherokees have so far become civilized as to appreciate a regular form of government...

DOCUMENT 3

Source: David Wilmot, Representative from Pennsylvania, *Congressional Globe*, February 8, 1847

Sir, I was in favor of the annexation of Texas, The democracy of the North, almost to a man, went for annexation. Yes, sir, here was an Empire, larger than France given up to slavery. Should the North make further concessions? Shall we give up free territory, the inheritance of free labor? Sir, the South has her share already: the installation for slavery was paid in advance...Now Sir, we are told that California is ours, that New Mexico is ours, won by the valor of our arms. They are free. Shall they remain free? Shall these fair provinces be the inheritance and homes of the white labor or freemen or the black labor of slaves? This, sir is the issue – this is the question. The North has the right and her representatives have the power.

But the South contends that, in their emigration to this free territory, they have the right to take and hold slaves, the same as other property…Slavery follows in the rear of our armies. Shall the war power of our government be exerted to produce such as result? Shall our government depart from its neutrality on this question, and lend its power and influence to plant slavery in these territories?

DOCUMENT 4

Source: Charles Sumner, Senator from Massachusetts, "Report on the War with Mexico," April 1847

It cannot be doubted that this is a war of conquest…It is a war for the extension of slavery over a territory which has already been purged, by Mexican authority, from this stain and curse. Fresh markets of human beings are to be established; further opportunities for this hateful traffic are to be opened; the lash of the overseer is to be quickened in new regions…a government professing the law of charity and justice, should be employed in a war to extend an institution which exists in defiance of these sacred principles. It has already been shown that the annexation of Texas was consummated for this purpose. The Mexican War is a countenance, a prolongation of the same efforts…

DOCUMENT 5

Source: William Seward, speech, "The Contest and the Crisis." 1855

An immediate issue involves the question whether Kansas shall be rescued from jeopardy of Slavery…and brought into the Union as a free state…

Slavery which is now firmly planted on the coast of Mexico, and which extends upward to the border of Kansas, will cross that border, and fasten its outposts on the southern border of British America. Thus the free States will be shut out from the Pacific coast. Divided by this wall…Slavery grasps the dominion of the Republic…Shall this be the inglorious end of the Republican system planted at Plymouth…this the inglorious end of the Republic delivered by Lafayette, organized by Hamilton, and consolidated by Washington?

DOCUMENT 6

Source: *The Independent* (Oskaloosa, Kansas), newspaper article, 1863

Under the beneficent provisions of the Homestead Act, thousands can find excellent lands on the line of the Railroad, and tens of thousands can select the most beautiful location all over Western Kansas.

Let this war be brought to a close, and we shall soon see these unoccupied lands made fruitful fields. In no place in the United States can such openings be found for settlement. As yet, but a very small proportion of the Government land is taken.

DOCUMENT 7

Source: Chauncey Depew (ed.), One Hundred Years of American Commerce, 1795 – 1895

RAILROAD MILEAGE INCREASE BY GROUPS OF STATES

Region	1850	1860	1870
New England	2,507	3,660	4,494
Middle States	3,202	6,705	10,964
Southern States	2,036	8,838	11,192
Western States and Territories	1,276	11,400	24,587
Pacific States and Territories		23	1,677
TOTALS	**9,021**	**30,626**	**52,914**

ANNOTATED PLAN B ESSAY

Western expansion had a significant effect on the development of the United States. Although western expansion enabled the United States to grow and prosper, it had tragic consequences for Native Americans while also inflaming sectional tensions over slavery.

> Thesis: The thesis makes a clear and defensible claim.

John L. O'Sullivan gave the American expansionist spirit a name when he coined the phrase "Manifest Destiny." In Document 1, "O'Sullivan confidently predicts that America "is destined to be the greatest nation of futurity," He hoped his widely read essays promoting Manifest Destiny would inspire waves of settlers to spread the advantages of American civilization into the West's great "untrodden space."

> Document 1 is accurately described.
>
> The discussion presents a valid Purpose analysis for Document 1.

The spirit of Manifest Destiny did not benefit everyone. Manifest Destiny failed to include a place for Native Americans. Cherokee tribes were the first to feel the impact of western expansion. In 1830, Congress passed the Indian Removal Act ordering eastern tribes to leave their homelands and move to the newly created Indian Territory in present-day Oklahoma. In Document 2, Elias Boudinot, an influential member of the Cherokee Tribe, accuses the "Great Father" Andrew Jackson of violating "the sacred obligations of treaties and laws." But his protests were in vain. Jackson's successor Martin van Buren ordered the forced evacuation of about 17,000 Cherokees. As many as a fourth of these people died on a tragic march now known as the Trail of Tears.

> Document 2 is accurately described.
>
> The discussion presents a valid Historic Situation analysis for Document 2.
>
> The discussion of the Trail of Tears is presented as relevant Outside Information.

The land acquired by the Mexican Cession opened the divisive question of the status of slavery in the western territories. Charles Sumner was a leading abolitionist. In Document 4 he foresaw how the annexation of Texts benefitted plantation owners instead of small farmers. He warned that the territorial gains from the Mexican-American War would soon be used for slave auctions. Sumner forcefully expresses the abolitionist point of view that the expansion of slavery into the western territories represents a betrayal of America's founding principle of liberty.

Document 4 is accurately described.

The discussion presents a valid Point of View analysis for Document 4.

COMMENTARY

This model Plan B essay would receive 4 rubric points. The essay opens with a clear thesis that establishes a defensible line of reasoning. Paragraphs 2, 3, and 4 accurately describe Documents 1, 2, and 4. Sourcing information is provided for each of these three documents. And finally, the essay provides relevant outside information for Document 2.

SCORING SUMMARY

THESIS	1 point	Paragraph 1 provides a clear and defensible thesis statement.
CONTEXTUALIZATION	0 points	The essay does not provide a broader historic context.
DOCUMENT CONTENT	1 point	The essay accurately describes the content of three documents.
EVIDENCE BEYOND THE DOCUMENTS	1 point	The discussion of the Trail of Tears provides relevant outside information.
ANALYSIS (HAPPY)	1 point	The essay identifies the purpose of Document 1, the historic situation for Document 2 and the point of view for Document 4.
COMPLEXITY	0 points	The essay does not meet the criteria required to earn the complexity point.
	4 points	

CHAPTER 15

PLAN B PRACTICE IMMIGRATION

Chapter 13 introduced and explained the Plan B strategy for earning 4 rubric points on your DBQ. This chapter is designed to provide you with an additional opportunity to practice your ability to write a Plan B DBQ essay.

PROMPT

Evaluate the relative importance of the effects of the waves of non-English groups who immigrated to America between 1840 and 1925.

DOCUMENT 1

Source: American Party (Know-Nothing Party) campaign pamphlet, 1854

America for the Americans! That is the watchword that should ring through the length and breadth of the land, from the lips of the whole people...

America for the Americans! We have had enough of Young Irelands, Young Germanys, and Young Italys. We have been patient but the time has come to right the wrong...

Americans must rule America! To this end native-born citizens should be selected to all state, federal, and municipal offices of government employment, in preference to all other.

DOCUMENT 2

Source: California Senate Special Committee on Chinese Immigration, 1878

The Chinese have now lived among us, in considerable numbers for a quarter of a century, and yet they remain separate, distinct from, and antagonistic to our people in thinking, mode of life, in tastes and principles, and are as far from assimilation as when they first arrived.

They fail to comprehend our system of government; they perform no duties of citizenship; they are not available as jurymen; cannot be called upon as a posse to preserve order, nor be relied upon as soldiers.

They do not comprehend or appreciate our social ideas, and they contribute but little to the support of our institutions, public or private.

We respectively submit that no nation, much less a republic, can safely permit the presence of a large and increasing element among its people which cannot be assimilated or made to comprehend the responsibilities of citizenship.

DOCUMENT 3

Source: Emma Lazarus, "The New Colossus," written in 1883, engraved on a bronze plaque mounted on the pedestal of the Statue of Liberty in 1903

Not like the brazen giant of Greek fame,

With conquering limbs astride from land to land;

Here at our sea-washed, sunset gates shall stand

A mighty woman with a torch, whose flame

Is the imprisoned lightning and her name

Mother of Exiles. From her beacon-hand

Glows world-wide welcome; her mild eyes command

The air-bridged harbor that twin cities frame.

"Keep, ancient lands, your storied pomp!" cries she

With silent lips. "Give me your tired, your poor,

Your huddled masses yearning to breathe free,

The wretched refuse of your teeming shore.

Send these, the homeless, tempest-tost to me,

I lift my lamp beside the golden door!"

DOCUMENT 4

Source: Israel Zangwill, The Melting Pot, 1909

America is God's Crucible, the great Melting Pot where all the races of Europe are melting and reforming! Here you stand good folk, think I, when I see them at Ellis Island, her you stand in your fifty groups with your fifty languages and histories, and your fifty blood hatreds and rivalries. But you won't be long like that, brothers, for these are the fires of God you've come to – these are the fires of God. A fig for your feuds and vendettas! Germans and Frenchmen, Irishmen and Englishmen, Jews and Russians – into the Crucible with you all! God is making an American.

DOCUMENT 5

Source: Edward A. Ross, Century Magazine, 1914

In 1908, on the occasion of a homecoming celebration in Boston, a newspaper told how the returning sons of Boston were greeted by Mayor Fitzgerald and the following members of Congress: O'Connell, Kelihar, Sullivan, and McNary following in the footsteps of Webster, Sumner, Adams, and Hoar. They were told of the great work as Mayor of the late beloved Patrick Collins. At the City Hall they found the sons of Irish exiles and immigrants administering the affairs of the metropolis of New England. Besides the Mayor, they were greeted by John J. Murphy, Chairman of the Board of Assessors; Commissioner of Streets Doyle; Commissioner of Baths O'Brien...Police Commissioner O'Meara.

DOCUMENT 6

Source: Madison Grant, The Passing of the Great Race, 1918

Whatever may be its intellectual, its literacy, its artistic or its musical aptitudes, as compared with other races, the Anglo-Saxon branch of the Nordic race is again showing itself to be that upon which the nation must chiefly depend for leadership, for courage, for loyalty, for unity and harmony of action, for self-sacrifice and devotion to an ideal. Not that members of other races are not doing their part, many of them are, but in no other human stock which has come to this country is there displayed the unanimity of heart, mind and action which is now being displayed by the descendants of the blue-eyed, fair-haired peoples of the north of Europe.

DOCUMENT 7

Source: Providence Evening Journal, "The Only Way to Handle It," 1921, Courtesy of Library of Congress

The Only Way to Handle It

ANNOTATED PLAN B ESSAY

America responded to each wave of non-English immigrants with a contradictory combination of welcome and rejection. During the period between 1840 and 1925, unfounded nativist fears ultimately dominated America's response as the United States banned Chinese immigrants and used restrictive quotas to sharply reduce the flow of immigrants from Southern and Eastern Europe.

Thesis: The thesis makes a clear and defensible claim.

During the 1840s the threat of starvation forced about 1.5 million Irish to leave their homeland and pour into port cities in the Northeast. Black-robed Chinese priests and nuns seemed strange and frightening to Protestant Americans. Alarmed native-born citizens formed the Know-Nothing Party to restrict Irish political participation. Document 1 provides an excerpt from a Know-Nothing campaign pamphlet. Written to encourage voters to support its candidates in the 1854 election, the pamphlet forcefully declared "Americans must rule America!" and that only native-born citizens should hold public office.

Document 1 is accurately described.

The discussion presents a valid Purpose analysis for Document 1.

Nativism was not limited to the East Coast. The discovery of gold in California and the availability of well-paying construction jobs on the transcontinental railroad attracted thousands of Chinese workers. The newcomers soon faced a wave of nativist resentment. Document 2 provides a list of grievances compiled by a Special California Senate Committee. The list was part of a national campaign intended to persuade Congress to restrict Chinese immigration into the United States. The nativist campaign worked. Although the Chinese constituted a tiny percentage of the United States population, nativist pressure

Document 2 is accurately described.

The discussion presents a valid Purpose analysis for Document 2.

persuaded Congress to pass the Chinese Exclusion Act of 1882. Signed into law by President Arthur, the act banned Chinese from entering the United States. The Chinese Exclusion Act marked America's first legislation targeting a specific racial group of immigrants.

The first two decades of the twentieth century witnessed a massive wave of Catholic and Jewish immigrants from Southern and Eastern Europe. These so-called "New Immigrants" sparked an intense national debate. Nativists exploited the climate of anxiety and suspicion caused by World War I and the Red Scare. The editorial cartoon in Document 7 expresses the nativist point of view that restrictive quotas were "the only way" to cut the flow of New Immigrants. Congress responded to nativist pressure by enacting the National Origins Act of 1924. As recommended by the cartoon in Document 7, the law used restrictive quotas to block the great wave of New Immigrants from entering America.

The discussion of the Chinese Exclusion Act is presented as relevant <u>Outside Information</u>.

Document 7 is accurately described.

The discussion presents a valid <u>Point of View</u> analysis for Document 7.

COMMENTARY

This model Plan B essay would receive 4 rubric points. The essay opens with a clear thesis that establishes a defensible line of reasoning. Paragraphs 2, 3, and 4 accurately describe Documents 1, 2, and 7. Sourcing information is provided for each of these three documents. And finally, the essay provides relevant outside information for Document 2.

SCORING SUMMARY

THESIS	1 point	Paragraph 1 provides a clear and defensible thesis statement.
CONTEXTUALIZATION	0 points	The essay does not provide a broader historic context.
DOCUMENT CONTENT	1 point	The essay accurately describes the content of three documents.
EVIDENCE BEYOND THE DOCUMENTS	1 point	The discussion of the Chinese Exclusion Act provides relevant outside information.
ANALYSIS (HAPPY)	1 point	The essay identifies the purpose of Documents 1 and 2 and the point of view of Document 7.
COMPLEXITY	0 points	The essay does not meet the criteria required to earn the complexity point.
	4 points	

CHAPTER 16

PLAN B PRACTICE FOREIGN POLICY 1900– 1940

Chapter 13 introduced and explained the Plan B strategy for earning 4 rubric points on your DBQ. This chapter is designed to provide you with an additional opportunity to practice your ability to write a Plan B DBQ essay.

PROMPT

Evaluate the extent of change in the global role of the United States from 1900 to 1940.

DOCUMENT 1

Source: Senator Henry Cabot Lodge, Sr., speech to the United States Senate Committee on Foreign Relations, August 12, 1919.

Mr. President:

The United States is the world's best hope, but if you fetter her in the interests and quarrels of other nations, if you tangle her in the intrigues of Europe, you will destroy her power for good and endanger her very existence....No doubt many excellent and patriotic people see coming fulfillment of noble ideals in the words "league for peace." We all respect and share these aspirations and desires, but some of us see no hope, but rather defeat, for them in this murky covenant. For we, too, have our ideals, even if we differ from those who have tried to establish a monopoly of idealism.

DOCUMENT 2

Source: *Puck*, "Columbia's Easter Bonnet," April 6, 1901
Courtesy Library of Congress

COLUMBIA'S EASTER BONNET.

DOCUMENT 3

Source: Alejandro Cesar, Nicaraguan representative to the United States, message regarding support for the military government in Nicaragua to Secretary of State Frank Billings Kellogg, 1927

After a long and unfortunate conflict [a civil war from 1926 – 1927] for the maintenance of order and the institutions of the Republic, the Nicaraguan Government views its war materials considerably diminished, and it is therefore obliged to restore its stocks of such materials at the earliest possible moment…. It therefore approaches your government confident that it will meet with the same … spirit of friendship which it has always found, and which has come to be proverbial in the relations between Nicaragua and the United States.

In view of the foregoing I take the liberty of expressing to you the desire of the Nicaraguan Government to enter into negotiations to secure war materials…. As soon as the general situation of the country is normalized, larger quantities and other classes of war materials will undoubtedly be required.

As soon as the necessity of completing the national armament is met, through the benevolent aid of the United States Government, the Nicaraguan Government will unfailingly attain the end of assuring the most precise conditions of peace and tranquility within the Republic and surely the people and government of Nicaragua will thereby contract a new debt of gratitude toward the people and Government of the United States.

DOCUMENT 4

Source: Edwin L. James, European correspondent of the *New York Times*, October 1930

Officially, our government stays out of world organizations… we continue to shy at the World Court. But such things count for less and less. We must deal with the world and the world must deal with us. Let there be an international conference, and imponderable influences bring the United States there. A conference on reparations, we are there. The International Bank is set up, an American is made president. The World Court meets, an American is put on the bench...

It is always the case that the American position is among the most important. Such is one of the prices of our power. Few world problems arise in which the influence of the United States will not swing the decision if we take a real interest. Opposition to the United States is a serious undertaking. Our dollars are powerful; there are so many of them.

DOCUMENT 5

Source: Neutrality Act of 1935

Resolved by the Senate and the House of Representatives of the United States of America assembled, That upon the outbreak or during the progress of war between, or among, two or more foreign states, the President shall proclaim such fact, and it shall thereafter be unlawful to export arms, ammunition, or implements of war from any place in the United States or possessions of the United States, to any port of such belligerent states, or to any neutral port for transshipment to, or for the use of, a belligerent country.

DOCUMENT 6

Source: President Franklin D. Roosevelt, Quarantine Speech, October 5, 1937

The peace-loving nations must make a concerted effort in opposition to those violations of treaties and those ignorings of humane instincts which today are creating a state of international anarchy and instability from which there is no escape through mere isolation or neutrality.

Those who cherish their freedom and recognize and respect the equal right of their neighbors to be free and live in peace must work together for the triumph of law and moral principles in order that peace, justice, and confidence may prevail in the world. There must be a return to a belief in the pledged word, in the value of a signed treaty. There must be recognition of the fact that national morality is as vital as private morality.

DOCUMENT 7

Source: Carey Orr, "The Only Way We Can Save Her," political cartoon, 1939

The Only Way We Can Save Her

ANNOTATED PLAN B ESSAY

During the four decades between 1900 and 1940, American foreign policy appeared to make dramatic shifts from intervention and imperialism to withdrawal and isolationism. Despite these changing policies, America inevitably pursued its national interest by playing an active role in global economic and political affairs.

Thesis: The thesis makes a clear and definitive claim.

The cartoon in Document 2 was published shortly after America's victory in the Spanish-American War. It portrays Columbia as a self-confident symbol of America. She is shown proudly adjusting an Easter Bonnet labelled "World Power." Bristling with powerful guns, the bonnet spews a cloud of thick black smoke labelled "Expansion." Columbia looks in a mirror and is clearly pleased with her image as a new imperial power. The cartoonist uses this confident image to express his support for America's position as a new world power. However, the cartoon ignores the ongoing Philippine Insurrection. This armed conflict between Philippine nationalists and the United States claimed thousands of lives and belied America's support for popular rule and national self-determination.

Document 2 is accurately described.

The discussion presents a valid Purpose analysis for Document 2.

The discussion of the Philippine Insurrection provides relevant Outside Information.

In Document 3, Alejandro Cesar, the Nicaraguan representative to the United States, formally requests that Secretary of State Kellogg approve the sale of military equipment to his country. At that time, the United States followed an isolationist foreign policy that included not joining the League of Nations while supporting the Washington Naval Conference's provisions to reduce the naval arms race in the Pacific. However, Cesar seems to assume that these policies did not apply to Central America. He was right. During

Document 3 is accurately described.

The discussion provides a valid Historic Setting and Point of View analysis for Document 3.

the 1920s, the United States continued to exercise military and economic influence in the region. For example, the U.S. sent marines and military equipment to support Nicaragua's unpopular but pro-American government.

Carey Orr published the cartoon in Document 7 in 1939. At that time, World War II had just erupted in Europe. The war divided America into two opposing camps - isolationists who wanted the United States to remain neutral and interventionists who wanted America to support its allies and oppose fascist aggression. The kneeling woman in Orr's cartoon symbolizes the United States. She is beseeching Uncle Sam to "Stay Out!" The symbolic figures and text convey Orr's point of view that America must stay out of "War Mad Europe" in order to preserve the United States as the "Last Refuge of Democracy."

Document 7 is accurately described.

The discussion provides a valid Historic Setting and Point of View analysis.

COMMENTARY

This model Plan B essay would receive 4 rubric points. The essay opens with a clear thesis that establishes a defensible line of reasoning. Paragraphs 2, 3, and 4 accurately describe Documents 2, 3, and 7. Sourcing information is provided for each of these three documents. And finally, the essay provides relevant outside information for Document 2.

SCORING SUMMARY

THESIS	1 point	Paragraph 1 provides a clear and defensible thesis statement.
CONTEXTUALIZATION	0 points	The essay does not provide a broader historic context.
DOCUMENT CONTENT	1 point	The essay accurately describes the content of three documents.
EVIDENCE BEYOND THE DOCUMENTS	1 point	The discussion of the Philippine Insurrection provides relevant outside information.
ANALYSIS (HAPPY)	1 point	The essay identifies the purpose of Document 2, the point of view of Documents 3 and 7, and the historic setting for Documents 3 and 7.
COMPLEXITY	0 points	The essay does not meet the criteria required to earn the complexity point.
	4 points	

Made in United States
North Haven, CT
26 December 2023

46640108R00078